"Aiming his interpretation at a broad array of readers, Moloney's book is inspired by the idea that Revelation is an 'Easter Book.' For Moloney, Revelation insists that Christians already enjoy full access to life through Jesus's death and resurrection, a helpful correction to those who may over-read the book's eschatology. Those less attuned to the minutiae of scholarship will find a readable introduction to the content of the book of Revelation. Moloney coordinates his interpretation of specific sections of Revelation with their place in the lectionary and liturgy of the hours, which provides a helpful guide for those who want to understand more fully how to interpret Revelation in a liturgical context."

— Micah Kiel
St. Ambrose University

"The distinguished Johannine scholar Fr. Francis Moloney, taking a cue from liturgy, has produced a guide to Revelation for the Office of Readings in weeks two through five after Easter. His interpretation is a striking departure from interpretations of Revelation as a coded sequence of disasters leading to the apocalypse, an earthly millennium, and heavenly paradise for the faithful who survived the tribulations. Instead Fr. Moloney insists that salvation was mediated through the death of the Lamb from the beginning of creation. The story being told in symbolic visions is that of faithful Israel preserved in the Jewish Scripture, an account of those who obeyed Torah and gave witness to God's messiah. Certainly a picture of salvation fully realized in the Easter proclamation is better suited to Revelation's liturgical use than apocalyptic horrors. Still Moloney's imaginative reconfiguration of almost everything Christians have thought about Revelation requires time and patience."

— Pheme Perkins
Boston College

D1428539

# Reading Revelation at Easter Time

*Francis J. Moloney, SDB*

**LITURGICAL PRESS**
Collegeville, Minnesota

www.litpress.org

1   2   3   4   5   6   7   8   9

**Library of Congress Cataloging-in-Publication Data**

Names: Moloney, Francis J., author.
Title: Reading Revelation at Easter time / Francis J. Moloney, SDB.
Description: Collegeville, Minnesota : Liturgical Press, [2020] | Includes bibliographical references. | Summary: "An exploration of the Book of Revelation as a celebration of the perennial and ongoing effects of Jesus' death and resurrection"—Provided by publisher.
Identifiers: LCCN 2019054018 (print) | LCCN 2019054019 (ebook) | ISBN 9780814685051 (paperback) | ISBN 9780814685297 (epub) | ISBN 9780814685297 (mobi) | ISBN 9780814685297 (pdf)
Subjects: LCSH: Bible. Revelation—Commentaries. | Bible. Revelation—Liturgical use. | Eastertide—Meditations.
Classification: LCC BS2825.53 .M655 2020 (print) | LCC BS2825.53 (ebook) | DDC 228/.07—dc23
LC record available at https://lccn.loc.gov/2019054018
LC ebook record available at https://lccn.loc.gov/2019054019

Believe what you read,
teach what you believe,
and practice what you preach.
(*Roman Ritual for the Ordination of a Deacon*)

# Contents

# Preface

The book of Revelation is the most challenging book in the New Testament. Most mainstream Christians do not read it, and some sectarian Christian groups have used the fierce and often threatening imagery as biblical judgment against individual people and institutions across the ages. This practice was passionately and widely used across all sides of the tragic and often violent divisions that shook the Christian church and society in general in the sixteenth century.[1] Some continue to use it as an inspired guide to what will happen at the end of all time, generating many different "millenarian" interpretations (see Rev 20:1-6). Unfortunately, some fanatical groups have done great damage to themselves and to an understanding of Christianity through a fundamentalist and fanatical "end-time" reading of the book of Revelation. Revelation is not a book for religious fanatics, but over the centuries such readings by Christians have kept it "in the news."

Despite its challenging nature, the Christian churches, especially in the Western world, use the book of Revelation in their

---

[1] The art of Lucas Cranach the Elder (1472–1553) and Albrecht Dürer (1474–1528) are eloquent testimonies of that era. However, they were not alone in graphically casting opposing Christian communities as the Antichrist, an expression that never appears in the book of Revelation. See Carlos M.N. Eire, *Reformations. The Early Modern World, 1450–1650* (New Haven, CT: Yale University Press, 2016), 178–84; Eamon Duffy, "Brush for Hire: Lucas Cranach the Elder," in *Royal Books and Holy Bones. Essays in Medieval Christianity* (London: Bloomsbury Continuum, 2018), 301–18.

liturgies. This is not the case in the Eastern churches, where a suspicion of its usefulness as a "word of God" has long existed. In the West the "Office of Readings," part of the official daily *Liturgy of the Hours* in the Roman tradition, uses passages from Revelation from the Second to the Fifth Weeks of the Easter season. The book is read sequentially, almost in its entirety. A similar focus upon the Easter relevance of Revelation appears in the selection of four passages as canticles at Evening Prayer for the days of the week, on Sundays, and other major feast days. Its use as a reading for the celebration of Mass over the final weekdays in the Year 2 Cycle of the Ordinary of the Year tends to accentuate a more conventional understanding of Revelation as pointing toward "the end." But even at that "eschatological" time of the liturgical year, the readings reflect God's victory in and through Jesus Christ. As is well known, Revelation 12's presentation of the woman clothed with the sun, the moon under her feet (Rev 12:1) has long been used for the Catholic celebration of Marian feasts, as has Revelation 7:2-4, 9-14 on the feast of All Saints. That passage tells evocatively of the gathering of the "saints" from the tribes of Israel, saved by the blood of the Lamb.

The presentation of the book of Revelation that follows will argue that the allocation of the book of Revelation as part of the church's Easter celebrations was an inspired decision.[2] What follows will suggest that the theme of the death and resurrection of Jesus Christ dominates Revelation. This is not a majority interpretation of this challenging New Testament book. In different ways, most interpret John's work as an encouragement of Christians, living through suffering and persecution, to hold tight to their Christian beliefs and practice.

---

[2] The allocation of texts from the book of Revelation for use in the *Liturgy of the Hours* and the celebration of the Eucharist continues age-old liturgical practice. See Andrew B. McGowan, *Ancient Christian Worship. Early Church Practices in Social, Historical, and Theological Perspective* (Grand Rapids, MI: Baker Academic, 2014), 80, 90, 219.

They are promised that, in the end, God will reward their faithfulness and punish the wicked. Although some suggest that this resolution of Christian pain, suffering, and death, will take place in a final establishment of God's kingdom *on earth*, most suggest that God's final intervention will take place *outside time and space*.

Under the shadow of that widespread (and somewhat frightening) understanding of the book of Revelation, rendered complex by outrageous symbols and difficult narrative sequences, most Christians regard it as incomprehensible. But an author, who reveals his name as "John" (see 1:1, 4, 9, 22:8), opens his book with a song of praise to Jesus Christ: "To him who loves us and freed us from our sins by his blood, and made us to be a kingdom, priests serving his God and Father, to him be glory and dominion forever and ever" (1:5b-6).[3] Taking our cue from John himself, reading the book of Revelation as an Easter book attempts to "make sense" of the book itself. Revelation has long been part of the Christian canon, the books the Christian churches regard as Sacred Scripture. It celebrates something that, in a Christian view of history, has already happened. Jesus Christ's death and resurrection is an event that determines the whole of time, from the foundation of the world to the present (see 13:8). The ancient Christian maxim *lex orandi lex credendi* strongly suggests that the consistent "praying" of Revelation on Sundays and during the Easter season is an articulation of the church's Easter "faith."

*Reading Revelation at Easter Time* attempts to unlock some of the book's secrets by suggesting that the key to its interpretation is locating Jesus Christ's death and resurrection at its theological and literary heart. Most Christians who come across Revelation in their prayers and liturgies are overwhelmed by its challenges. Many turn away from these strange readings,

---

[3] Citations from the biblical text come from the NRSV (New Revised Standard Version) translation. Occasionally I will use my own translation, indicated by the abbreviation AT (author's translation).

replacing them with works of more immediate personal or community relevance. I hope to ease those tendencies by providing ten brief chapters that divide John's text into identifiable literary units, reflecting upon them in the sequence that appears in the *Liturgy of the Hours*, following the narrative flow of Revelation 1:1–22:21. I attempt to "make sense" of the narrative of the book of Revelation for those who follow its day-by-day appearance from the Second till the Fifth Week of Easter.

## *Dual Typefaces*

I trust that many will read this book from the first to the last page, but it has been designed and written to accompany the readings that appear in the *Liturgy of the Hours* across the Easter period. The foreign nature of the book of Revelation demands patient commitment, without trying to bite off too much at any one time. Out of respect for the allocation of the readings from Revelation across the Easter period, some "bites" run for a few pages, while others are longer. Given the use of texts from Revelation at places in the church's liturgy that fall outside Easter time, I provided an appendix to this book, listing all the occurrences of the book of Revelation in the Roman liturgy, as a guide to where a commentary on them can be found. Within the book a different typeface is used for commentaries on these passages, with an appropriate note indicating where the passages are used. Thus, the liturgical use of Revelation outside the Office of Readings will be identified but embedded in their context in the book's unfolding narrative. However, the church's steady use of Revelation from the Second to the Fifth Weeks of the Easter season in the *Liturgy of the Hours* determines the structure of the book.

What follows is a simplification of my large scholarly commentary upon the book of Revelation, *The Apocalypse of John. A Commentary*, published in Grand Rapids, Michigan, by Baker Academic in 2020. Heavily dependent upon the research behind that study, I am deeply grateful to all at Baker Academic who have graciously allowed me to produce this book for a more general audience. The commentary on the book of Revelation remains the same, but I have eliminated almost all scholarly discussion, and focused on a reading that, in my opinion, "makes Easter sense."

I am responding to requests from several Roman Catholic pastors who asked me to provide a guide through the confusing pages of Revelation. Engagement with the scholarly academy that has led me to the following reading of the book of Revelation is found in my *The Apocalypse of John. A Commentary*. None of that is called for in this present study. As I celebrate the fiftieth anniversary of my own priestly ordination (July 11, 1970), I offer this brief book, focused upon the *Liturgy of the Hours*, to all Christian pastors, in the hope that it might shed "Easter light" upon their ministry of the Word. The words on the dedication page, taken from the Roman Rite for the Ordination of a Deacon, is a brotherly reminder to all of us.

Francis J. Moloney, SDB, AM, FAHA
Catholic Theological College, University of Divinity,
Melbourne, Victoria, Australia

# CHAPTER ONE

## Introduction:
## Hope in Challenging Times

As we begin our Easter journey through the book of Revelation, some introductory issues must be faced, as many contemporary commentators regard Revelation text as directed to Asian Christians, identified in the seven letters found in 2:1–3:22, who are suffering persecution, and even martyrdom, because of their Christian beliefs. In this view, the use of powerful images, clothed in highly symbolic and sometimes unimaginable language, tells of the mysterious but inevitable intervention of God at the end of time. Late in the first and into the second Christian centuries, Jews and Christians developed an abundant form of literature classified as "apocalyptic." Such literature had already appeared in the Old Testament, especially in the book of Daniel that appeared in mid-160 CE, during a time of severe persecution in Israel. In general terms, apocalyptic literature addresses communities that are facing difficulties that no human endeavor can reverse. Apocalypses are at one-and-the-same-time earthly, because they address a human situation, and other-worldly, because divine intervention into human suffering resolves the crisis.

For traditional Christian apocalyptic readings of Revelation, *in the end* God will punish and destroy the wicked, while the persevering faithful will be victorious. In more technical terms, the conflict between the good and the wicked is resolved by

God's *eschatological intervention*, a decisive "end of human history" event. The reading that follows insists that *Revelation should not be interpreted as a traditional Jewish Christian "apocalypse."*[1] Although John (see 1:1, 4, 9; 22:8) uses many of the literary features of Jewish apocalypses, he was convinced that Jesus, the slain Lamb (see 5:6; 13:8), has been raised. God's saving entry into human history was not something that would happen in the future, and perhaps outside our time and space. It has already happened in the death and resurrection of the slain Lamb (see 1:5-8, 9-20; 5:5-6, 9-14; 7:9-17; 8:1; 10:7; 11:15-19; 16:17; 17:1-18; 19:11–20:15). John believes that Christians *already enjoy* access to life because of the death and resurrection of Jesus. It is hardly Christian to ask believers to wait, and perhaps suffer and die, across a period that will lead to God's final intervention. Revelation, despite the literary form that it borrows from Jewish apocalyptic literature, is a Christian reflection on Israel's Sacred Scriptures, especially the prophets Ezekiel and Daniel.

## *Date and Author*

Since late in the second Christian century, especially under the influence of Irenaeus's *Against Heresies* 5.30.3 (ca. 180 CE), the book of Revelation has been associated with the latter years of the Emperor Domitian (Emperor: 81–96 CE). It is possible that the author used traditions from across fifty years, from the 60s until the end of the first century CE, to create the book of

---

[1] I am aware that I may create confusion by insisting that the book of Revelation is not a Jewish Christian "apocalypse." The book itself is often called "The Apocalypse," taking that title from its very first Greek word: *apokalypsis*. The word means "revelation" (and thus the book is regularly called "Revelation"). The book is about the revelation of Jesus Christ (Rev 1:1) and has many characteristics that come from a literary form called "apocalyptic." But, as I will insist, despite its literary form, it does not *function* as an apocalypse: disclosing the secrets that will mark the end of time. For more detail on this, see Sherri Brown and Francis J. Moloney, *Interpreting the New Testament. An Introduction* (Grand Rapids, MI: Eerdmans, 2019), 214–35.

Revelation as we have it in our Bibles. Justin Martyr (100–165 CE. See his *Dialogue with Trypho* 81.4) already regarded the book as part of early Christian literature. From the time of Irenaeus (ca. 180 CE), the author has been identified with the apostle, John the son of Zebedee. But this identification has always been queried, given the obscurity and complexity of the book (Gaius: early third century CE; Dionysius of Alexandria: latter half of the third century). It differed too radically from the Johannine gospel and letters. The first Christian church historian, Eusebius, reports the views of Gaius and Dionysius, and indicated similar doubts in the fourth book of his *Historia ecclesiastica* early in the fourth century CE (ca. 322–326 CE).

Nowadays, most would claim that it is not possible for us to identify the person and the role of the author with any precision. The author names himself "John," and this claim should be accepted. His presence on Patmos was the result of his Christian missionary activity. He was not necessarily a prisoner there. David Aune, one of the most significant contemporary commentators on the book of Revelation identifies the author as follows:

> While the final author-editor of Revelation was named "John," it is not possible to identify him with any other early Christian figures of the same name, including John the son of Zebedee or the shadowy figure of John the Elder. The otherwise unknown author of Revelation in its final form was probably a Palestinian Jew who had emigrated to the Roman province of Asia. . . . He regarded himself as a Christian prophet.[2]

The Jewishness of John is strikingly evident in his extraordinary use of the Sacred Scriptures of Israel, and his familiarity with the literary forms of Jewish apocalyptic. The text of the

---

[2] David E. Aune, *Revelation*, 3 vols., Word Biblical Commentary 52A-C (Dallas: Word, 1997–1998), 1:lvi. I have modified Aune's description by eliminating his identification of the author as a Jew fleeing during the first Jewish revolt in 66–70 CE. This cannot be proven.

book of Revelation is full of repeated allusions to the Scriptures, especially the Torah, Isaiah, Ezekiel, and Daniel. However, unlike other early Christian authors, John never cites his biblical sources. But his literary world is entirely Jewish.

## *Literary Genre*

After the salutation of 1:1-3, Jesus Christ is presented in the prologue to the document as the firstborn from among the dead, and the ruler of priests and kings on earth (vv. 4-5). The audience hears letters to seven Asian churches, which may have a deeper meaning than seven letters of exhortation and warnings to the churches (2:1–3:22). Behind the letters the audience senses allusions to Israel's sacred history, from the primeval history of Genesis (2:4-5, 7) to Christ, standing at the door, knocking (3:20). The promises made to the victors across the letters (see 2:7, 11, 17, 26-28; 3:5, 12, 21) may be an appeal to the audience to be a truly Christian people and church, "a kingdom of priests, serving his God and Father" (1:6). Many of the promises to the victors in the letters of 2:1–3:22 return in the description and the role of the New Jerusalem in 21:9–22:5. Perhaps John makes promises to the church in 2:1–3:22 and describes the fulfillment of those promises in 21:9–22:5.

The letters are followed by the vision of a solemn liturgy that takes place in heaven (4:1–5:15). The climax of that vision is the appearance of a Lamb, already victorious: slain yet standing (5:6). The heavenly court sings his praise, recognizing that his death has ransomed all humankind (5:9-14). *Because of this* he is "worthy to take the scroll and open its seals" (v. 9). The Lamb receives universal praise and worship (vv. 11-14). The "narrative" has only just begun, yet John has proclaimed that the slain yet standing Lamb is victorious.

This victory is told again as each seven closes. It is found in the silence that marks the opening of the seventh seal (8:1) marking the end of the period from creation to Jesus' death and resurrection (see 7:1-8), and the establishment of a period of universal salvation enabled by that death and resurrection (7:9-17). It is promised in the blowing of the sixth trumpet that "in the days when the seventh angel is to blow his trumpet, the mystery of God will be fulfilled" (10:7). Then, the blowing of the seventh trumpet results in the opening of God's temple, as "the kingdom of the world has become the kingdom of our Lord and of his Messiah" (11:15-19).

After a long preparation, addressing the ambiguity of the human condition (12:1-18), describing the action of Satan's agents in spreading evil (13:1-18), and God's initial intervention on behalf of the saints of Israel (14:1-20), the seven bowls are poured out. Prefaced by a heavenly encounter, the lines are drawn for battle (15:1–16:21). The battle of Harmagedon (16:16) tells of the definitive conflict between good and evil at the cross of Jesus Christ. The victory is once more announced: "It is done!" (16:17).

The consequences of this definitive victory are then spelled out in detail. Babylon is destroyed (17:1–19:10), all evil power is definitively eliminated by God's victory in the death and resurrection of Jesus (19:11–20:15). The chosen ones are gathered into the messianic kingdom that may not be "other-worldly," but a God-given Christian community (21:1–22:5). The audience of Revelation is not given a road map to God's other-worldly eschatological victory but is roundly and repeatedly instructed that life and light have been made available for the New Jerusalem, the Christian community as it should be, through the death and resurrection of Jesus Christ (see 22:1-5). John repeatedly affirms that the victory has already been won by "the Lamb who was slain since the foundation of the world" (13:8 AT).

## A Christian Apocalypse?

Craig Koester points out that Revelation departs from the usual pattern of apocalyptic literature. He states that "the eschatological struggle had already begun with the Messiah's exaltation and would culminate at his return. Those events define the present time."[3] But this does not explain John's repeated claim that the decisive victory *has already been won*: "It is done!" (16:17). It is not "in process," but has been realized in the perennially available saving action of God in the death and resurrection of Jesus. Its fruits are found in the New Jerusalem, the Christian church (see 21:1–22:5).

No doubt the recipients of John's book of Revelation faced difficulties. Many of these difficulties were created by the widespread influence of the Greco-Roman religious practices within the powerful political presence of the Roman Empire. Some of them, if we are to judge by what is said to the seven churches (see 2:4, 14-16, 20-23; 3:1-3, 15-16), arise from the fragility of their own commitment. But John's primary concern is not to exhort Christians to wait in faith and hope for God's final eschatological victory. The document is studded, from beginning to end, with proclamations of the victory of God from all time in and through the slain and risen Lamb (see 1:5-8, 9-20; 5:5-6, 9-14; 7:9-17; 8:1; 10:7; 11:15-19; 16:17, 17:1-18; 19:11–20:15). There must be a tension, as in all Christian literature, between what God has already achieved in and through Jesus Christ, and his final return (see 22:20). But the decisive victory has been won. God's saving history, revealed throughout Israel's story and in the Christian church, rejoices in what God has done for humankind across history in and through the saving effects of the death and resurrection of Jesus Christ, from before the foundation of the world (see 5:6; 13:8).

Although John tells the recipients of Revelation what God has *already* achieved, they are nevertheless exhorted to call out: "Come, Lord Jesus!" (22:20). They are exhorted to live confidently in the glitter of a Greco-Roman world, aware of the saving effects of the death and resurrection of Jesus. Nevertheless, they must still face the challenges of a world marked

[3] Craig R. Koester, *Revelation*, Anchor Yale Bible 38A (New Haven, CT: Yale University Press, 2014), 107.

by the ambiguous presence of grace and sin: "Let the evildoer still do evil, and the filthy still be filthy, and the righteous still do right, and the holy still be holy" (22:11. See also vv. 14-15). Such ambiguity will be finally resolved only when the Lord Jesus comes (22:20).[4]

## A Christian Prophecy

John regards his work as prophecy (1:3; 19:10; 22:7, 10, 18, 19). He has been given a commission to prophesy (10:11). A link with traditional biblical prophecy is certainly a feature of John's practice of interlacing his narrative with allusions to the biblical prophets, especially Isaiah, Ezekiel, and Daniel. The Hebrew Bible, and not the speculations of Jewish or Jewish-Christian apocalyptic, forms the essential literary backbone to Revelation, even though it is never directly cited.

Early Christians sometimes understood a "prophet" as a prolongation of the spirit of traditional prophecy, making a link with both the Hebrew Bible and the message of Jesus. As M. Eugene Boring puts it: "Christian prophets were thus those who spoke the message of the risen Lord directly to the Christian community."[5] John's prophetic utterances address Christians at the end of the first century with the message of the saving effects of the death and resurrection of Jesus. The prophetic nature of Revelation disqualifies it as a traditional apocalypse.

---

[4] The theme of the coexistence of good and evil is regularly stated across Revelation. Appearing first in the Prologue, repeated across the "sevens," it returns with considerable force in the Epilogue. See 1:7 (Prologue); 2:1–3:22 (the letters); 6:15-17 (sixth seal); 9:20-21 (sixth trumpet); 16:8-9 (fifth bowl), 10-11 (sixth bowl), 21 (seventh bowl); 18:4 (fallen Babylon); 21:7-8 (exclusion from the New Earth), 27 (exclusion from the New Jerusalem); 22:11, 14 (Epilogue).

[5] M. Eugene Boring, *Revelation*, Interpretation (Louisville, KY: John Knox Press, 1989), 25.

## Genre Bending

Harold W. Attridge suggests that the author of the Fourth Gospel regularly used traditional literary genres that lead an audience to expect usual outcomes. But he "bends" them, thus taking an audience into unexpected and unexplored possibilities.[6] He describes the practice as follows:

> In many cases where it is possible to identify significant generic parallels, and therefore presume that the form in question generates regular expectations, the reader encounters something quite odd about the way in which the generic conventions seem to work.[7]

John's marriage of prophetic and apocalyptic literary forms, including some letters, "bends" an audience's expectations. An author of apocalyptic literature envisions an end-time salvation. For John the victory has already been won, and the gift of the heavenly Jerusalem refers to the earthly reality of the Christian church. The key to the genre bending in Revelation is the death and resurrection of Jesus of Nazareth, a consequence of the incarnation, an event that took place once and for all within a human story. For John this event transformed human history, from the beginning of time till the present age (see 13:8). It is the center point of God's perennial saving presence, giving meaning to the whole of human history.

## Background and Literary Structure

In 1:9 John describes his role as a prophetic missionary, witness to the word of God and Jesus Christ. There is no evidence, apart from a prejudiced interpretation of 1:9, that Patmos was a penal colony. "John is the only person known to be sent

---

[6] Harold W. Attridge, "Genre Bending in the Fourth Gospel," *Journal of Biblical Literature* 121 (2002): 1–21.

[7] Attridge, "Genre Bending," 11.

there."[8] Domitian never systematically persecuted Christians.[9] Emperor worship in Asia was widespread, but evidence for the persecution of the Asian Christians for lack of observance of its cults is hard to find.[10] As Ramsey MacMullen puts it: "Had the church been wiped off the face of the earth at the end of the first century, its disappearance would have caused no dislocation in the empire, just as its presence was hardly noticed at the time. . . . Simply, it did not count."[11]

The seven churches of Asia, recipients of the letters in 2:1–3:22, are a symbol of the whole church (the number 7 indicates completeness). John challenges the church to live a Christian way of life in Greco-Roman society. Interpreters do not agree on the identity of people and problems mentioned in the letters (e.g. Nicolaitans, Antipas, Jezebel, Balaam, Balak, and the synagogue of Satan). It is equally difficult to identify why certain strengths and failures are credited to given communities, and not to others. In the light of the "seven mountains on which the woman is seated" (17:9), "Babylon the Great" is regularly identified with Rome, but it addresses the now destroyed former Jerusalem, unfaithful Israel, "drunk with the blood of the saints and the blood of the witnesses to Jesus" (17:6).[12] The "New Jerusalem," faithful Israel understood by John as the Christian church, replaces the former Jerusalem (Babylon).

Within that world, an Easter reading of Revelation can be outlined. Its central message is that the death and resurrection of Jesus reveal the meaning of the history of God's intervention into the affairs of humankind, recorded in the period of Israel

[8] Koester, *Revelation*, 239.

[9] See Leonard L. Thompson, *The Book of Revelation. Apocalypse and Empire* (New York: Oxford University Press, 1990), 107–115.

[10] See Steven J. Friesen, *Imperial Cults and the Apocalypse of John. Reading Revelation in the Ruins* (New York: Oxford University Press, 2001).

[11] Ramsey MacMullen, *Christianizing the Roman Empire (A.D. 100–400)* (New Haven, CT: Yale University Press, 1984), viii.

[12] We will see in our reflection upon Revelation 17:9 that the Jewish First Book of Enoch describes Jerusalem as situated on seven mountains. See below, p. 138.

and the period of the Christian community. It is a sacred history running from the foundation of the world to the time of the church. This message is repeated several times, with the use of "sevens" that determine its shape and message. Each "seven" is introduced by a description of heavenly encounters (1:9-20; 4:1–5:14; 8:2-6; 15:1-8). The pouring out of the seven bowls, the climactic announcement of Jesus' victory through death and resurrection, receives the most extensive treatment (12:1–22:25).

1:1–8: Prologue: The revelation of God and Christ.

> 1:9–3:22: Heavenly encounters [1:9-20] and the **seven letters** of the risen Christ to the churches [2:1–3:22].

4:1–8:1: Heavenly encounters [4:1–5:14] and the opening of the **seven seals** [6:1–8:1].

8:2–11:19: Heavenly encounters [8:2-6] and the blowing of the **seven trumpets** [8:7–11:19].

12:1–22:5: Pouring out the **seven bowls**:

> 12:1–14:20: *Threefold preparation for the pouring out of the bowls*: (1) The human situation [12:1-17]; (2) Political and religious corruption [13:1-18]; (3) Judgment [14:1-20].

15:1–16:21: Heavenly encounters [15:1-8] and the pouring out of the **seven bowls** [16:1-21].

> 17:1–21:8: *Threefold consequences of the pouring out of the bowls*: (1) The Destruction of Babylon (Jerusalem) [17:1–19:10]; (2) the final battle [19:11–21:8]; (3) the gift of the New Jerusalem [21:9–22:5].

22:6–21: Epilogue: Worship God, Come Lord Jesus.

There are surprises at every turn. Even though John is moved to communicate with his audience within the political, religious, and social presence of the Roman Empire, he does not limit his criticism to Rome. Inspired by Daniel's critique of all who have brought corruption and evil into Israel's history, his concern is to indicate that the death and resurrection of Jesus is a victory over *all* evil powers, and *all* false gods. The figure of the woman (*hē gunē*) looms large. Despite her glorious first appearance (12:1), by the time the passage closes in vv. 17-18, she and her descendants are in an ambiguous situation, pursued by Satan, but protected by God. In 17:1-6, mounted on the beast, her ambiguity has disappeared. The woman has made her decision to enter an unholy union with evil. But that is not the end of her story. She returns as the bride of the Lamb in 21:1–22:5.

Such readings are possible because the battle of Harmagedon in 16:1-21 should be understood as the crucifixion of Jesus, fulfilling what was promised in 10:7: "In the days when the seventh angel is to blow his trumpet, the mystery of God will be fulfilled, as he announced to his servants the prophets." In the crucifixion of Jesus, the pouring out of the seventh bowl, "It is done!" (16:17), a definitive victory over evil that has already been described in the opening of the seventh seal (8:1) and the blowing of the seventh trumpet (11:15-19).

Revelation is to be read as a steady statement and restatement of the saving effects of the death and resurrection of Jesus Christ, acting from before all time (5:6; 13:8), a call to live through challenge, conflict, suffering, and failure, in the light of the victory of the Lamb. The book is a celebration of the perennial significance of the death and resurrection of Jesus, the mystery of God's presence across the whole of sacred history, from the beginning of creation down to the time of the Christian church.

## Further Questions

Revelation is directed to Christians facing a situation of great ambiguity, caught between belief in the saving effects of the death and resurrection of Jesus and the allure of the glittering Greco-Roman world within which they lived. They are not experiencing persecution and death at the hands of the Emperor Domitian, nor are they being forced into emperor worship. Nevertheless, a "theology of resistance" is part of John's message, driven by the proclamation of the perennial saving presence of God in the death and resurrection of Jesus.

If Patmos was never a penal colony, Domitian was not persecuting Christians, and they were not being forced into emperor worship, why is there so much violent suffering depicted across the pages of the book of Revelation? Those who have suffered are regularly referred to as "the saints" (see 8:3-4; 11:18; 13:7, 10; 14:12; 16:6; 17:6; 18:20, 24; 19:8; 20:6, 9). John looks back to the recent past to the "Saints of the Most High," those holy ones of Israel who were loyal to the commandments of God, and placed their hopes in the messianic promises of the prophets (see Dan 7:21, 25, 27; 9:5-6a, 10).

## Who Are "the Saints"?

John's biblical allusions draw from across many pages of the Hebrew Scriptures, especially (but not only) the Torah, Isaiah, Ezekiel, and Daniel. His regular reference to those who suffer and are slain for the word of God and the messianic promises of the prophets (see 1:2, 9; 6:9; 12:17; 18:24; 19:10; 20:4) as "saints" comes from the era before the historical events of the death and resurrection of Jesus Christ, especially the experiences and vindication of the suffering and slain "saints" reported in the book of Daniel that emerged during the time of the persecutions of Antiochus IV (167–165 BCE). As Steve Moyise puts it: "Whether they were facing actual persecution or not, it seems clear that John wishes them to see their situation in the light of the life and death struggle of Daniel and his friends."[13]

[13] Steve Moyise, *The Old Testament in the Book of Revelation*, Supplements to the Journal for the Study of the New Testament 115 (Sheffield: Sheffield Academic Press, 1995), 58.

The literary character of the prophet Daniel played admirably into John's argument. On the one hand, the literary fiction created by Daniel sets the tales across the four empires of the Babylonians (Dan 1–5), the Medes (6:1), the Persians (10:1), and the Greeks (10:20). The earlier chapters (Dan 1–6) do not necessarily refer to the period of Antiochus IV. They convey a message of persecution of Jewish saints across the entirety of its history under political and religious tyranny. Across Daniel 7–12, allusions to the period of Antiochus IV and the Maccabean period are clear. The book of Daniel appeared between 167–164 BCE. By the time John wrote the book of Revelation, Daniel was exercising considerable influence in Jewish literature. The Jewish historian Josephus regarded Daniel as "one of the greatest prophets" (*Jewish Antiquities* 10.266).[14]

Sharply aware of the recent persecution and executions under Antiochus IV, John can address his early Christian audience by looking back to the prophet Daniel, claiming that the "saints" of Israel had already participated in the death and resurrection of Jesus throughout the nation's sacred history. Daniel indicates why this happened: they observed the commandments and listened to the prophets (see Dan 9:5–6, 10. See also Bar 1:14–2:5; 3:1-8). We cannot be sure, but John's continual recourse to Daniel may well have been the reason for the choice of the apocalyptic genre for his document, however much he has "bent" the genre because of his focus upon the death and resurrection of Jesus. For John, Israel's "saints" (see especially Dan 7:15-27) anticipated eternal redemption

---

[14] H. St. J. Thackeray, Ralph Markus, Allen Wikgren, Louis H. Feldman, eds. *Josephus*, 9 vols., The Loeb Classical Library (Cambridge, MA/London: Harvard University Press/William Heinemann, 1926–65), 6:305. Josephus (37–100 CE), a former leader in the Jewish revolt of 66–70 CE, joined the Romans and provided a remarkable, even though biased, account of the Jewish War (*The Jewish War*), and a retelling of Israel's sacred story (*Jewish Antiquities*).

provided by the blood of the crucified and risen Lamb, "slain before the foundation of the world" (13:8 AT).[15]

## Consequences

At the heart of John's message lies the perennial and saving effects of Jesus' death and resurrection. Corrupt political and religious tyranny led to the life-giving participation of the saints across the whole of Israel's religious and political history, from Babylon to Rome. The presence of the satanic did not begin or end with Rome, however much the Roman Empire and the Imperial Cult would have impacted upon John's audience. A history of corruption, rejection of God, and persecution has marked the whole span of Israel's history. But it has always been marked by the presence of its "saints." What does this say to late-first-century Christians? Does Revelation speak to Christians living in the third millennium?

John exhorts Christians living in the Greco-Roman world of the late first century to shun the immoral and commercial glitter of that world, aware that they already enjoy the life given by God in and through the death and resurrection of his Son. John was neither a starry-eyed apocalyptic thinker, nor someone who thought that Christians already lived the glories of the risen life (see 1 Cor 15:20-58). Like all other early Christian writers, he faced the ambiguous reality of Christians called to live their lives in imitation of the crucified and risen one within a socio-political-religious context that radically opposed such a lifestyle.

---

[15] This is the obvious translation of the Greek, but the NRSV translates: "everyone whose name has not been written from the foundation of the world in the book of life of the lamb that was slaughtered." Many commentators regard the notion of the Lamb being slain *before* the foundation of the world as "logically and theologically impossible" (Aune, *Revelation*, 2:747). They are unable to accept the obvious meaning of the Greek because they fail to see the unique *theological* contribution John makes to Christian thought. Abandoning the measure of linear time, John has his own logic.

All post-Christ believers live the in-between-time, negotiating its ambiguity. John exhorts his audience to look back upon the "endurance" of the saints in the face of devastating evil that was part of Israel's sacred history, the result of the fall of humankind and the fall of Satan (see 14:12). Demonic disasters challenge humankind, and creation itself, as a result of those "falls." But from the foundation of the world, redemption by the blood of the slaughtered lamb is available (5:6; 13:8). For John, those who observed the Law and listened to the messianic prophecies, *already in the period prior to the historical event of Jesus Christ*, were swept into that redemption.[16] John encourages his early Christians to shun the false promises of the demonic world that still surrounds them, as they await God's final appearance. The world of false promises and its agents have not disappeared because of the death and resurrection of Jesus, as the ambiguity of Christian history itself indicates so eloquently.

Living the in-between-time, Christians cry out, "Come, Lord Jesus!" (22:20). John wrote his book to instruct them that they had every reason for courage and confidence as they lived their Christian lives in the expectation of a final coming. John attempts to focus a Christian community, aware of the allusive possibilities of apocalyptic language, upon the vividly remembered treasure of the holy ones of Israel. "Christians lived quiet lives, not much different from other provincials. The economy, as always, had its ups and downs; and the government kept the peace and demanded taxes."[17] This situation, however,

---

[16] The icon used for the cover of this book, chosen from the widespread iconographic theme of the *Anastasis*, portrays the risen Jesus' *descensio ad inferos* ("descent into hell"). He leads Adam and Eve into glory by taking their hands, as Old Testament kings and prophets look on. The artistic tradition is associated with the *temporal*, an indication of what happened in the silence of Holy Saturday (see 8:1). It can also be understood as a portrayal of the *transtemporal* saving effects of Jesus' death and resurrection "from the foundation of the world" (13:8).

[17] Thompson, *Book of Revelation*, 95. See also pp. 164–67.

could easily lead to an uncritical accommodation of the traditions and *mores* of the Greco-Roman world.

Such a way of life is unacceptable in the Christian church, the perfection of God's promises, founded upon the death and resurrection of Jesus. John writes to make his audience aware, and to encourage them, by telling them that the faithfulness required of those who live in the blessedness of the post-Christ era had already been lived by people who were faithful unto death in the period between the original "fall" of Satan and humankind (see 9:1-2; 12:7-12) and the death and resurrection of Jesus (16:1-21). The victory of the saints of Israel, already participating in the death and resurrection of Jesus, was the result of their obedience to the Law and their belief in the messianic promises of the prophets. They are already gathered in glory (see 6:9-11; 7:1-8; 14:1; 15:1; 20:1-6). They share in "the first resurrection. . . . Over these the second death has no power, but they will be priests of God and of Christ, and they shall reign with him for a thousand years" (20:5c-6).[18] John used this message to address early Christians living the challenges of their time during which access to God was no longer through a temple in Jerusalem, but through the temple of the Lord God Almighty and the Lamb (21:22). Despite its challenges for a reader in the third millennium, John's Easter message retains its urgency, and fittingly closes the Christian Bible.

---

[18] This interpretation of the "thousand years reign" as the period of Israel, prior to the unleashing of Satan for the final battle of Jesus' death and resurrection, challenges almost all interpretations of Revelation 20:1-6. The thousand years do not indicate a precise chronological period that will mark the end of the Christian era, but the long period that elapsed between the original fall of Satan (see 9:1-2; 12:7-12) and his return only to be vanquished definitively by Jesus' death and resurrection (16:1-21). The passage has troubled interpreters from the beginnings of Christianity. To this day many Christian traditions are determined by their interpretation of the nature and timing of the "thousand-year reign": amillenarian, premillenarian, postmillenarian, and dispensationalist. For a good survey, explaining these terms, see Koester, *Revelation*, 741–50.

# CHAPTER TWO

## *Second Week of Easter: Monday through Thursday*

### Making Sense of Revelation 1:1–3:22

Revelation 1:1-8 is a self-contained prologue to the book, composed of an opening statement (vv. 1-3), and a greeting (vv. 4-8). In v. 9 John begins to speak of his personal experience on the island of Patmos. After his heavenly encounter (1:9-20), the seven letters, to Ephesus (2:1-7), Smyrna (2:8-11), Pergamum (2:12-17), Thyatira (2:18-29), Sardis (3:1-6), Philadelphia (3:7-13), and Laodicea (3:14-22), follow. The *Liturgy of the Hours* offers the prologue and the initial heavenly encounter (1:1-20) on the Monday of the Second Week of Easter (1:1-20), and the letters to the churches for the Tuesday (2:1-11), Wednesday (2:12-29), and Thursday (3:1-22).

## MONDAY

Throughout this book I will regularly indicate the structure of the passages we are considering. In this way we follow the author's literary design. Revelation 1:1-8 has two parts. In vv. 1-3 the book is introduced as God's revelation of Jesus Christ, through the mediation of the servant of a former era (the angel), and the servants of a new age (John and the recipients of the Revelation). The prologue closes in vv. 4-8, with the Easter message of grace and peace from God, the seven spirits, and the affirmation of the coming of the Christ, by God, the Alpha and the Omega, the Lord of all history.

## God's mediated revelation of Jesus Christ (1:1-3)

The first word of the book indicates that what follows is a "revelation," a gift from God consigned to Jesus Christ. God is the origin of the revelation of Jesus Christ, directed to Christian believers, God's servants (v. 1a). Jesus Christ is the one "to whom" God has entrusted his revelation. Thus, the revelation begins in God, is entrusted to Jesus Christ, and reaches its goal when received by humankind. But the revelation is mediated: "[H]e made it known by sending his angel to his servant John" (v. 1b). The book manifests what God has done in and through Jesus Christ. Jesus Christ executes God's design in a revelation that will happen unexpectedly, like the thief that comes in the night (see Matt 24:43; Rev 3:3; 16:15). It "must happen" (v. 1a. See Matt 26:54). Revelation 1:1 is an indication of "how" God intervenes—quickly (Greek: *en tachei*).[1]

There are two "times" across the book of Revelation. The former is a "time" when John receives revelations from the angel, "signs" that come from Israel's history, a revelation that looks back to God's presence prior to the death and resurrection of Jesus. However, as there is only one sacred history, with God as its Alpha and Omega (see v. 8), the "time" of Israel, mediated through an angel, looks forward to the fulfillment of Israel's messianic hopes: God's definitive saving action in the death and resurrection of Jesus, the testimony of Jesus

---

[1] Most critics claim that God will intervene "soon." The following reading of the book of Revelation always reads the Greek word *tachus* as an indication of "how" God will intervene ("quickly"), not "when" ("very soon"). Both are possible renditions of the Greek. See Frederick W. Danker, *Greek-English Lexicon of the New Testament and Other Early Christian Literature* (Chicago: University of Chicago Press, 2000), 992, under the word *tacheōs*, §1.

Christ (v. 2). Angels communicate Israel's anticipation of the death and resurrection of Jesus. John claims to be a recipient of God's design made known to Israel: the revelation of God in her Scriptures (v. 2a: "the word of God"), and the witness they give to the messianic hope (v. 2b: "the witness of Jesus Christ").

The recipient of John's writing is blessed; she or he is the recipient of an authoritative revelation that provides a key that opens the mystery of God's saving history. They are to live by it, as the opportune time (Greek: *kairos*) for this revelation is at hand (v. 3): the "divine opportunity" of God's visitation in the death and resurrection of Jesus. The first three verses of the prologue have tersely spelled out that God has consigned his revealing action to Jesus Christ. This action makes sense of God's intervention in the story of Israel and in the period of the church: the word of God and the testimony of Jesus Christ.

## *The coming of the Christ (1:4-8)*

The author "John" writes to the "seven churches" in the Province of Asia. The churches in Asia addressed by the letters of 2:1–3:22 are located in today's western Turkey. John chooses "seven" to indicate that the letters are addressed to the whole church. The traditional greeting of grace and peace come from a divinity described as "he who is and who was, and who is coming" (AT), a clear reference to the biblical God (see Exod 3:14: "I AM WHO I AM"). John uses the present tense (Greek: *ho erchomenos*) to further describe God as "he who is coming." The transcendent God of Israel from always ("who is and who was"), linked with the world ("is coming"), is the active presence of God across the whole of salvation history.[2]

---

[2] On the Jewish use of the expression "he who is, who was, and is coming," developing God's revelation of "the name of God" in Exodus 3:13-15, see Richard Bauckham, *The Theology of the Book of Revelation*, New Testament Theology (Cambridge: Cambridge University Press, 1993), 28–30.

The image of the "seven" spirits who are before the throne of God comes to John from Zechariah 4:1-14, a passage from the Hebrew Bible associated with the restoration of the Jerusalem temple after Israel's return from exile in 539 BCE. Zechariah sees a lampstand, with seven lamps upon it. He asks an angel to explain what they signify. After assuring him with the authority of the Lord that the restored temple will come not "by power, but by my spirit" (Zech 4:6), the meaning of the lamps is provided: "These seven are the eyes of the LORD, which range through the whole earth" (v. 10). For John, the seven spirits are a complete manifestation of the Spirit. They belong to God, as they are "before his throne" (Rev 1:4). Spirits that belong to God will reach out to humankind, in a fashion that parallels Zechariah's description of them as "the eyes of the LORD, which range through the whole earth" (Zech 4:10). For the moment, they are part of John's primitive presentation of a "trinity": a transcendent God, seven divine spirits before the throne of God, and Jesus Christ. John asks that grace and peace be poured out upon those who receive his document from God, the spirits, and Jesus Christ.

A rich development of the role and person of Jesus Christ, much of which comes to John from the Jewish Scriptures, emerges in vv. 5-6. The rhythm of "three" continues into the description of Jesus Christ. First, John describes Jesus Christ as one who is "the faithful witness" and he "who loves us." John also points out that he is the crucified and risen one: "the firstborn of the dead." Finally, the fruits of this life, death, and resurrection are that Jesus Christ "has freed us from our sins by his blood" (v. 5). He is established as "the ruler of the kings of the earth" (v. 5), and he has "made us to be a kingdom, priests serving his God and Father" (v. 6). As if responding to this praise, the text takes on the form of a hymn to progress into a further threefold description in v. 7 of Jesus Christ's person, his action, and their consequences. He is the Messiah: "He is coming with the clouds" (v. 7a. See Dan 7:13), who will be executed and who will rise: "Every eye will see him, even those who pierced him" (v. 7b. See Zech 12:10ab). Finally, he effects judgment upon humankind: "On his account all the tribes of the earth will wail" (v. 7b. See Zech 12:10c-14).

The prologue of Revelation 1:1-8 closes with the voice of God, indicating that only God makes sense of the whole of history, from its beginning (Alpha) to its end (Omega) (v. 8). The Lord God transcends all time and creation, but has always been intimately involved in the human story through his "coming" (v. 8). John's belief that two sacred times formed God's saving history is hinted at in 1:1-8 (see v. 2: "the word of God" and "the testimony of Jesus Christ"). Through the mediation of an angel and the prophet John, the God of all history (v. 8: Alpha and Omega) reveals through his word and the testimony of his Son that the death and resurrection of Jesus Christ has brought judgment and has established a kingdom of priests. The audience, already part of that kingdom, owes eternal glory and praise to him.

## *Heavenly encounters (1:9-20)*[3]

John *hears* "a loud voice like a trumpet" from behind (vv. 10-11). Upon turning he *sees* one like a Son of Man face-to-face (vv. 12-16). He *speaks* to John, commanding him to *write* (vv. 17-20). John's initial experiences reflect the two moments of the revelation of God in and through Jesus Christ: in Israel's story and in the life of the Christian church.

### *The voice from behind, like a trumpet: The revelation of God's initial saving intervention (1:9-11)*

John is a "brother" to his recipients. Patmos was not a center for punishment. As Craig Koester remarks: "John is the

---

[3] Revelation 1:9-11a, 12-13, 17-19 provides the second reading in the Liturgy of the Word for the Second Sunday of Easter in Year C. See above, p. xviii, for an explanation of the change in typeface.

only person known to have been sent there."[4] On an island not too distant from the Asian churches, John associates himself with Ezekiel and Daniel, two "prophets" who were portrayed as prophesying in the exile of Babylon. John is present in Patmos as a prophetic missionary, driven by a passion *for the word of God and a courageous witness to Jesus Christ.*[5] He shares the suffering, the kingdom, and the patient endurance with his readers and listeners because of his faithfulness to both the Law ("the word of God") and to the messianic prophecies ("testimony to Jesus"). In this, he is a product of a belief in what God has done across the story of Israel, as he lives and proclaims the word of God (Torah). He also gives witness to the coming of Jesus Christ, witnessed to in the messianic hope of Israel (witness to Jesus; v. 9).

John further describes himself as "in the Spirit," and "on the Lord's day." The fact that his auditory and visual experiences took place on the Lord's Day associates them with the day of the resurrection of Jesus Christ. Illuminated by the Spirit he prophetically unfolds mysteries and communicates them to others. Within this prophetic setting, repeating the experience of the prophet Ezekiel (Ezek 3:12-13), he hears the loud voice, like a trumpet, coming from behind him. Across Revelation the "loud voice" is the voice of an angel (see 5:2, 11; 7:2; 8:13; 10:3). Recalling God's communication with the faithful by means of an angel from the prologue (v. 1b), this first encounter locates John within the experience of God's people, sharing the experience of the prophet Ezekiel, receiving a communication that takes place through an angel. Trumpets are always associated with revelation in the Hebrew Bible, as they were associated with the gift of the Law on Sinai (see Exod 19:16-19; 20:18. See also 2 Sam 6:15; Ps 47:5; Joel 2:1; Zech 9:14; Heb 12:19).

---

[4] Koester, *Revelation*, 243.
[5] See also Thompson, *Book of Revelation*, 172–73.

In vv. 9-11, an angel communicates to a human agent (John) that he must take on a prophetic mission: write what he sees to the seven churches. The communication of the revelation of God through an angel is indirect, associated with the voice of an angel that sounds like a trumpet. John must communicate to the churches, named in v. 11, the prophetic revelation of the saving promises made to Israel. The message to the churches, however, cannot only tell the story of God's intervention in Israel. The Sacred Scriptures of Israel find their explanation, their perfection, in the revelation of God that takes place in and through the death and resurrection of Jesus Christ.

## *The sight of one speaking:*
## *The revelation of God's definitive intervention (1:12-20)*

The story of God's presence to Israel and in the Christian church are part of one divine design, and both receive the fullness of their meaning from the death and resurrection of Jesus Christ, the consummation of the former and the beginning of the latter. There is only one revelation of Jesus Christ (v. 1a), but it has two phases, one across the story of Israel (vv. 9-11) and another in the church (vv. 12-20), one the perfection of the earlier promises. John must share both moments of God's revealing history with the church ("seven churches"). The voice, first heard in v. 10, leads John to turn in order to "see the voice" that spoke. "Hearing" turns into "sight." John does not see a person speaking; he sees seven golden lampstands (v. 12). John's first "sight" is related to God's chosen people and their cult: lampstands. There are seven of them, and they are golden. The seven lampstands indicate the fullness of the cult of Israel, and their being made of gold associates them with the divine.

John then sees that they are associated with "one like the Son of Man," located in the midst of the seven golden lampstands (v. 13). He walks in the heart of the cult of Israel, suggesting that the book will go on to reveal the perennial "coming" of Christ through the story of Israel, now fulfilled in the church: "the seven lampstands are the seven churches" (v. 20). This vision of the seven churches reveals communities called to complete God's design for the cult of Israel, in which the risen Christ has always been present. In vv. 13-15 the clothing, hair, feet, and the sound of the voice of this figure are described in a free association of imagery used to describe God and the Son of Man in Daniel 7:9-10, 13-14; 10:5-10; and Ezekiel 1:27. The combination of these prophecies singles out the one like a Son of Man as a divine messianic figure, completing God's design for the cult of Israel.

The voice of the Son of Man is not like a trumpet, as was the voice as reported in v. 10, but "like the sound of many waters" (v. 15). This is a further allusion to the book of Ezekiel: "And there, the glory of the God of Israel was coming from the east; the sound was *like the sound of many waters*" (Ezek 43:2 AT). For John, "the many waters" indicates that the voice of the Son of Man is directed to "peoples and multitudes and nations and languages" (17:15. See 5:9; 7:9; 17:1). The voice like a trumpet was directed to the prophetic figure of John the Seer who was called to announce to the churches the significance of the story of Israel that leads to the death and resurrection of Jesus Christ (vv. 10-11). The voice of the Son of Man, "like the sound of many waters," indicates the universal effects of the situation established through the death and resurrection of Jesus. The revelatory and judging role of the word of the one like Son of Man is indicated by the image of the sharp two-edged sword coming from his mouth (v. 16b), and the divine authority of that revelation and judgment is seen in his face, shining like the sun with full force (v. 16c).

His right hand holds seven stars (v. 16a). This information is provided without explanation, but the use of "seven" indicates to the audience that the stars are associated with fullness and completion. In his right hand they are under his authority and protection. John falls to his face at his feet, as though dead (v. 17. See Dan 10:9; Ezek 1:28. See also Dan 8:17). The prophets Daniel and Ezekiel fell, but not "as though dead" (Rev 1:17). They were exhorted to get back on their feet again (Dan 10:10; Ezek 2:1). John re-reads and enriches this imagery as he is summoned back to life by the right hand of one like a Son of Man on his shoulder, insisting, in language that recalls the theophanies of the Hebrew Scriptures, that he should not fear (Rev 1:17ab). The one like a Son of Man raises him. John now reports the one like a Son of Man's direct communication with him.

John's audience, aware of the difference between the experiences of Ezekiel and John, senses a hint of the resurrection of the believer resulting from the intervention of Jesus Christ. Not only does the one like a Son of Man raise John and speak as God speaks (see Gen 15:1; 26:24; 46:3; Isa 41:13-24; 43:1, 5; Dan 10:12: "Do not be afraid"), but he also announces the source of his authority. Repeating the claim of v. 8, that he is Lord of all history, the first and the last, the death and resurrection of Jesus Christ are explicitly announced for the first time: he is "the living one." He was dead, and now he is alive, and he lives forever and ever. As such, death no longer has any authority over him; he holds the keys to death and Hades (v. 18).

Lord of all history, the result of his death and resurrection, now alive, the one like a Son of Man holds the keys to death and Hades. The one who has overcome death is the Lord of death and its cruel consequences (Hades). The raising of the prostrate John is but proof of that truth (v. 17). What God has done in and through the death and resurrection of Jesus makes sense of the whole of salvation history: Jesus Christ is the first and the last. This is the message John must write, based upon what he has already experienced, and what is yet to come in the narrative that follows: his entire visionary experience (v. 19).

The one like a Son of Man, the crucified and risen Jesus Christ, is still speaking, as he will continue to speak, without interruption, through the dictation of the letters to the seven churches, the seven stars in his right hand (vv. 16-17, 20). God's design for the completion of Jewish cult, represented by the seven lampstands, is found in the seven churches, an image of the church as such. John "wishes to say that with the coming of Jesus Christ, Judaism and its cult and spiritual heritage have become the church."[6]

# TUESDAY

## *The seven churches (2:1–3:22)*

All seven letters have a similar literary pattern:

a)  Introduction:
    i. Address
    ii. Presentation of Christ as the one who sends the letter

b)  Body of the letter:
    i. Praise, correction, warning, and advice to the churches
    ii. Honoring the coming of Christ

c)  Conclusion:
    i. An invitation to listen to the voice of the Spirit
    ii. Promises to the victor

The Christian communities addressed by the letters most likely reflect historical churches known to John. He describes himself as "your brother," most likely "brethren" generated during his missionary experiences (see 1:9). He raises genuine problems the church faced, living its young Christian experience in the religious and secular reality of the Greco-Roman world. However, across the letters he inserts a sweeping sketch of God's saving interventions in the biblical story, based on allusions to

---

[6] Eugenio Corsini, *The Apocalypse of John. The Perennial Revelation of Jesus Christ,* trans. and ed. Francis J. Moloney (Eugene, OR: Wipf & Stock, 2019 [Reprint of 1983 original]), 94.

the biblical saga, from the Genesis account of an abandoned initial love (see 2:4) to the one like a Son of Man standing at the door, seeking entrance (3:20). The speaker is always the one like a Son of Man, but each church is addressed by its angel (2:1, 8, 12, 18, 3:1, 7, 14). They are part of a Jewish idea of an angelic heavenly representative for each church.[7] Bearing the authority of the one like a Son of Man, these angelic scribes (2:1, 8, 12, 18; 3:1, 7, 14: "write") tell a narrative of Israel's sacred history, the long messianic preparation for the Christian community. The seven letters represent Israel's sacred story, foreshadowing, preparing, and instructing the church, *as well as* being concrete exhortation and warnings to the church in Asia.

## *Ephesus: The fall from original love (2:1-7)*

The angel of Ephesus is to write a description of Christ taken from 1:20: "[H]im who holds the seven stars in his right hand, who walks among the seven golden lampstands" (2:1). The body of the letter praises the community for its endurance in difficulty, for its rejection of evil people, and for testing the claims of false apostles. It has not grown weary (vv. 2-3). It also recognizes that the Ephesians have hated the practices of the Nicolaitans (v. 6). We have no idea who the Nicolaitans were. However, all is not perfect: "You have abandoned the love you had at first" (v. 4). Unless they recognize their fall and repent from this situation and return to their original love, Christ will come and remove the lampstand from its place (v. 5). As with all the letters, they are summoned to listen to what the Spirit is saying to the churches, and the Ephesians are promised who do so will conquer, and the one like a Son of Man "will give permission to eat from the tree of life that is in the paradise of God" (v. 7).

---

[7] See Boring, *Revelation*, 86: "Just as each nation has its representative 'angel' in the heavenly world (cf. e.g., Dan 10:2-14, 20-21), so each congregation has its representative 'guardian' angel in the heavenly world."

Christianity must endure in a hostile world, reject evil and false claims, repent of practices hated by Christ. These challenges were real. But their abandoning the love they had at first alludes to the original fall of humankind (2:4. See Gen 3), and its consequences: work, toil, and endurance (v. 3. See Gen 3:16-19). They are instructed to look back upon this decisive moment of the breach in the oneness between God and humankind: "Remember then from what you have fallen" (v. 5). The account of humankind's fall is indicated by the promise made to those who conquer: "I will give permission to eat from the tree of life that is in the paradise of God" (v. 7. See Gen 2:15-17; 3:1-7).

## Smyrna: Affliction and the plagues in Egypt (2:8-11)

The angel of the church in Smyrna presents Christ in terms that are taken from 1:17-18: "the words of the first and the last, who was dead and came to life" (2:8). The situation of the church is one of rejection, hardship, poverty, and slander from "those who say they are Jews and are not, but are a synagogue of Satan" (v. 9). The church is exhorted not to fear in the face of oncoming suffering, imprisonment, testing and "ten days" of affliction. They are to be faithful unto death, and the victor will be given "the crown of life" (v. 10). Anyone who listens to what the Spirit is saying to the churches "will not be harmed by the second death" (v. 11).

Early Christian communities suffered from rejection by their religious "parent," Judaism. John suggests that the presence of the synagogue does not represent a people of God, but a synagogue of Satan (v. 9). The presentation of the synagogue in Smyrna as having lost its way, and having fallen into the clutches of Satan, is John's literary and polemical participation in the deeply felt, and emotionally articulated, tension that existed between Christians and Jews before, during, and after the "parting of the ways." We are not able to identify the exact nature of the rejection, hardship, and imprisonment that John associates with the church in Smyrna. But John rejects a form of Judaism that has historically not recognized Jesus of Nazareth as the Messiah announced by the Scriptures (see, for example, Rom 9:6; John 16:2).

There is a subtle link between the situation in Smyrna and Israel's experience in Egypt. Under Joseph, the Egyptians showed love and generosity (see Gen 50:15-26; Exod 1:1-7). This turned to hatred and slavery (Exod 1:8-14). The "ten days" of affliction alludes to the ten plagues which were endured by both Egypt and Israel in the days that led to the exodus (Exod 7:14–12:42). Israel was freed by the hand of God. Both Egypt of old and the Jewish community in Smyrna are a "synagogue of Satan" (v. 9), allowing themselves to be seduced from God's purposes to become persecutors and murderers. As in Egypt, even though they suffer, are slain, and imprisoned, Christ will give the victor "the crown of life" (v. 10). Those who listen to what the Spirit is saying to the churches will not be harmed by the "second death" (v. 11). The reference to the "second death" will be clarified later in the narrative (see 20:11-15; 21:8). But the audience is made aware from the beginning of the story that faithful listening to the word of God will lead to an avoidance of a negative judgment.

# WEDNESDAY

## *Pergamum: Israel in the desert "where Satan's throne is" (2:12-17)*

The angel of Pergamum looks back to 1:16 for his presentation of Christ as "the words of him who has the sharp two-edged sword" (2:12). The church is praised for holding fast to the name of the Christ, not denying faith in him, not even in the days when one of the faithful, Antipas, was slain (vv. 13b-14). They live in a dangerous situation, the place where Satan's throne is established (vv. 13ac). The throne of Satan could be established in any of the cities that were religiously, economically, and politically dominated by a Greco-Roman culture. Satan sits on his throne in that place where God should be king. Among them are unidentifiable people with the names Balaam, whose teaching taught Balak "to put a stumbling block before the people of Israel," leading them to eat food sacrificed to idols and practice fornication (v. 14). The problem of the Nicolaitans in the letter to Ephesus returns, a further indication that the description of possible failure in the letters deals with the same problems across all seven churches (v. 15. See v. 6). Repentance is called for, lest the judging two-edged sword in the mouth of Christ will come quickly and make war against them (v. 16. See 1:16). Problems facing a young church in the Greco-Roman world, "where Satan's throne is" (v. 13), continue to be listed, as the church in Pergamum is congratulated for holding fast to the faith, even in the face of the execution of one of its members.

The historical experience of an Asian church no doubt lies behind the letter, including the name of an executed Christian, Antipas. But being lured into fornication and eating food sacrificed to idols as a result of the influence of Balaam on Balak is more than factual reporting. Similarly, the one listening to the voice of the Spirit to the churches, and the one who conquers is promised "hidden manna" and a white stone, bearing a new name that only the one who receives it will know. These are clear references to the next stage of Israel's experience of God's saving history: her presence in the desert, after the liberation, and crossing the Red Sea.

The desert is traditionally a place of temptation, a fact that might enable John to speak of "the place" where Satan is established (v. 13). The use of the otherwise unidentifiable characters, Balaam and Balak, recalls the episode in the desert where the Lord overcame collusion between Balaam and Balak to deceive the Israelites (v. 14. See Num 22:1–25:25; 31:16). Moses looks back on the incident as a moment of treachery: "Behold, these caused the people of Israel, by the counsel of Balaam, to act treacherously against the Lord" (Num 31:16 AT). The attributed fornication and eating food sacrificed to idols (v. 14) looks back to the consistent danger of Israel's worshipping of false gods in the desert, especially the golden calf incident (Exod 32-34, especially 34:15-18 where the Israelites are accused of committing "fornication"), and the desire to return to the food of Egypt (Exod 16:1-4; Num 11:1-6, and *passim*). The enigmatic "white stone" with a name written on it (v. 17b) may allude to the two stones, bearing the names of the tribes of Israel, which the high priest carried on the shoulders of the Ephod (Exod 28:9-14). The "hidden manna" (v. 17a) summons the memory of Exodus 16:13-36.

## *Thyatira: Sinful rulers in Israel (2:18-29)*

The angel of Thyatira also recalls the heavenly introduction to the letters in the description of Christ as "the Son of God, who has eyes like a flame of fire, and whose feet are like burnished bronze" (v. 2:18. See 1:14-15).[8] This community is praised for its many good works: love, faith, service, and constancy, and these works continue to grow and flourish (v. 19). Nevertheless, a figure named Jezebel is present in the community. Acting as a prophet, she is calling the believers to the practice of fornication and the eating of food sacrificed to idols (v. 20). Christ warns that he has given her time for repentance. As this has had no effect, Jezebel, her lovers, and her children (who will be slain) will be subjected to severe punishment (vv. 21-23a). This punishment will instruct all the churches that Christ is the one who searches the mind and gives each of them what they deserve (v. 23b).

They are not to be part of disorders described as "the deep things of Satan," continuing the satanic theme from the letter to Pergamum (see 2:13). No further burdens will be laid upon

---

[8] This is the only time in Revelation that John applies the term "the Son of God" to Jesus Christ.

them; they must maintain that endurance for which they were initially praised: "[H]old fast to what you have until I come" (vv. 24-25. See v. 19). The concrete experiences of a young Christian church in the Greco-Roman world continue: virtue and strength in the midst of false prophecies leading to idolatrous practices that parallel those described in the church at Pergamum, a widespread challenge for these early churches (see 2:14; 1 Cor 8-10). The judgment of such practices lies ahead, and all the churches must recognize that Christian truth (vv. 23b, 25). To the one who conquers, Christ promises power over the nations, described in a paraphrase of Psalm 2:9: "to rule them with an iron rod." The victorious faith will be given "the morning star" (vv. 26-28).

An allusion to the time of Israel's kings is clear. This was a time of increasing wealth, expansion, and power, as with the virtue of the church at Thyatira (v. 19. See 1 Kgs 1:47). Solomon ruled during the height of this period (968–928 CE). But it led to material and spiritual corruption (see 11:1-8). The use of the name "Jezebel" in v. 20 links John's narrative to the period. She was the cruel wife of Ahab, the power behind the throne (873–852 BCE). She was also a foreign idolatress in the nation (16:31). At her instigation Ahab sees to the slaying of Naboth (21:1-14), and the prophecy of Elijah against Ahab and his wife matches the destiny of her lovers and children (21:17-24. See Rev 2:22-23). This prophecy also spells out the end of the Davidic rule: "In his son's days I will bring the disaster on his house" (1 Kgs 21:29). The letter to Thyatira addresses problems of the first-century church in Asia, but allusion to the biblical record of God's dealings with Israel is also present. From a position of royal strength came the seeds of religious corruption and eventual political destruction. God's word, through his prophet, makes this known. It is only the faithful believers who will have authority over the nations, and "rule with an iron rod" (Rev 2:27). Such authority, although promised to a Davidic king in Psalm 2:9, was eventually taken from Israel's royal line, as the prophet Elijah promised in 1 Kings 21:29. The message to Thyatira began by identifying Christ as the royal Son of God, and it concludes by promising that the faithful will share in his reign (2:26-28).

# THURSDAY

## *Sardis: The end of Israel and Judah, with a small remnant remaining (3:1-6)*

The angel of Sardis describes Christ as "him who has the seven spirits and the seven stars" (3:1), forging a link with the prologue (see 1:4: "seven spirits") and the heavenly introduction to the letters (see 1:16, 20: "seven stars"). The accusations against the community at Sardis are severe: they are living only by name. In reality they are dead. Within this dead community dwells a small group, but they are also on the point of death. Christ exhorts the whole church to wake up, to strengthen the small weak group that remains if they wish to be "perfect" in the sight of God (v. 2). They must recall what they have received and heard. They have a "name," but they do not live up to it (v. 1). Without repentance Christ will come upon them like a thief (v. 3). The message then turns to the small group in Sardis that remains. They are worthy. They have not soiled their clothes; they will walk with Christ, dressed in white (v. 4). The one who conquers will be clothed in white robes, and his "name" will not be blotted out from the book of life (v. 5). The empty "name" of v. 1 will be restored to a "name" in the book of life.

Continuing his allusions to the biblical saga of Israel's sacred history, John has generated the letter to Sardis, addressing contemporary problems of weakness and mediocrity of Christians within a Greco-Roman socio-religious context. But the imagery and message of the letter is based upon the state of desolation and death that followed the destruction of the kingdoms of Israel and Judah. God's chosen people were as if dead, reduced to a "remnant," a small group struggling to remain faithful (v. 2). This could apply equally well to Third Isaiah's more generic "remnant of Israel" (see Isa 65:8-10), and the vision of the life emerging from dry bones in Ezekiel 37:1-14, addressed to the exiles in Babylon during this period. In John's allusion to this period, the remnant is represented by "the few persons" who are worthy (Rev 3:4).

## Philadelphia: Return of a weak Israel and rebuilding the temple (3:7-13)

The angel of Philadelphia describes Christ as "the holy one, the true one, who has the key of David, who opens and no one will shut, who shuts and no one opens" (3:7. See Isa 22:22). The body of the letter asks the Philadelphians to look upon an open door that is before them. No one shall shut it (3:8a). The community is small and weak, but it has kept the word and not denied the name of Christ (v. 8). Continuing to address the Jewish community as "the synagogue of Satan" (see 2:9), Christ announces that some of them will see in their faithfulness to the word and the name of Christ that he has loved them. They will recognize that their rejection and execution of Jesus was the result of a lie and will join the Christian community (v. 9). Because of the Philadelphians' faithfulness to the word and their endurance, which has born such fruit, they will be kept "from the hour of temptation" that will visit the whole of the world and its inhabitants (v. 10 AT).

Christ announces that he is "coming quickly" (AT), and invites the community to keep what it already has, "that no one may seize your crown" (v. 11 AT). The victor is promised he will be placed like a column in the temple of God to which he will always belong (v. 13), and will have the names of Christ, the Father, and the heavenly Jerusalem written upon it (v. 12). Although not a feature of the early Christian movement, the possibility that the witness of the Christians might attract some of the local Jewish community must have always been a hope.

The earliest Christians saw themselves, in various ways, as the continuation of God's promises to Israel (see, for example, Rom 9–11). This attitude generated tension between Christian and Jewish communities.

A striking feature of this letter is the steady reference to a building: construction (v. 8), keys (v. 7), door (v. 8), column in the temple (v. 12), city of God (v. 12), the New Jerusalem (v. 12), the "name" of God, and of Jesus, which will be written on the pillar in the temple of God (v. 12). The community itself has "little power" (v. 8). In its weakness, the community is praised for its faithfulness and its perseverance in faith. These are allusions to the return from exile, the poverty and fragility of the returned community, the struggle to rebuild the temple, the temptation to give up in the light of their difficulties, frustrated by the surrounding Jewish community, regarded by John as unfaithful to their vocation as God's people (v. 9: "who say that they are Jews but are not"). The books of Ezra and Nehemiah tell this story, bringing the biblical record of Israel's saga to the threshold of the time of Jesus Christ. The "hour of trial" is coming to test the whole world and all the inhabitants of the earth (v. 10).

## Laodicea: Israel's rejection of their Messiah and the coming of the Son of Man (3:14-22)

The angel of the church announces Christ to the church in Laodicea as "the Amen, the faithful and true witness, the origin of God's creation" (v. 3:14. See Isa 65:15). Only in this letter does Christ find nothing good in the community. They are described as lukewarm, fit only to be spat out (vv. 15-16), vain but unhappy (v. 17a), wretched, deserving of pity, and poor, blind and naked (v. 17b). But they are given advice as to how they might overcome this situation. A loving Christ is at hand and calls them to repentance (v. 19). They are to buy gold refined by fire, white clothes for their nakedness, and ointment to cure their blindness (v. 18). The need for these possessions that only Christ can provide is urgent, as repentance is demanded (v. 19b), for "I am standing at the door, knocking; if you hear my voice and open the door, I will come in to you and eat with you, and you with me" (v. 20). The gold, white clothing, and ointment from Christ will reverse their situation entirely, as they will welcome and share with the one who is standing at the door. The one who conquers will be associated with Christ on his throne, matching the victory of Christ himself that enabled him to sit on the throne of his Father (v. 21). For the final time Christ warns: "Let anyone who has an ear listen to what the Spirit is saying to the churches" (v. 22).

Christ's vigorous condemnation of the Christians at Laodicea, associated with a loving call to repentance and reception of healing remedies that will lead them into an intimacy, exceeds any other church. They will share table with the one who stands at the door, and share Christ's throne, as his victory enabled him to share his Father's throne. Christian communities may have been guilty of lukewarmness, and thus fit only to be spat out (vv. 15-16). They may have been falsely proud of their wealth and possessions, but fundamentally unhappy (v. 17a), wretched, deserving of pity, and poor, blind and naked (v. 17b). But the letter to the church at Laodicea calls for an interpretation of Christ's accusations that extends beyond a critique of their pitiful Christian performance. After all, to the victors he promises a place beside him on his throne (v. 21).

John's message is harsh, but no harsher than a long history of Israel's own self-criticism through the prophets, or the ultimately condemnatory account of its history. The letter to Laodicea continues and develops that tradition. The lukewarmness is not some form of spiritual apathy. It is located in their claim to be the true people of God, yet not recognizing his Son. They offer praise to God and with all the external signs that accompanied God's promises to Israel, but that was no longer sufficient. They have not accepted what was promised. They are neither hot nor cold. The message from Christ, through their angel, is that he will spew them out (vv. 15-16).

In their claim to be rich and prosperous, needing nothing, they have in fact lost everything in their rejection of Jesus. They are "wretched, pitiable, poor, blind, and naked" (v. 17). But this is not the end. They are given "counsels" in vv. 18-19. In Revelation, gold is closely associated with the divinity (see 1:12: golden lampstands; 1:13: gold sash on the one like a Son of Man). Historical Israel is urged to recognize the divine in Christ, by purchasing gold from him. Not just any gold, but a gold that is pure, without sully and refined by fire (see Ps 18:31; Prov 30:5). This is an invitation to accept Jesus Christ, purified like gold from the fire of his death. Similarly, "white garments" in Revelation will always be used to refer to the new life that comes from an acceptance of Jesus. Finally, they are told to "salve and anoint your eyes that you may see" (v. 18).

There is a chance of newness of life, if only they will repent from their former ways, and accept the Christ whom they have slain (v. 19). With the letter to Laodicea, the audience arrives at the patient word of Jesus Christ that has been unfolding across the seven letters, through creation, history, Law and prophets. His advent is now close: "Listen! I am standing at the door, knocking; if you hear my voice and open the door, I will come in to you and eat with you, and you with me" (v. 20). These words are an invitation to Israel to come and take their place at the messianic banquet, at the wedding feast of the Lamb that lies ahead of the experience of the audience (see chapter 21). But they must hear the voice of Christ and open the door (v. 3:20). The stumbling block of the person of Jesus the Messiah must be overcome. For John, himself most likely a Jewish Christian, too many refuse Jesus' request. He regards them as people who say that they are Jews, but they are not. They are a synagogue of Satan (see v. 2:9; v. 3:9).

The letters have indicated that Israel's story promises a definitive access to God. But choices must be made, and this is the point of the promises made to the victors at the close of each letter. Each in its own way promises participation in God's messianic kingdom (2:7, 10, 11, 17, 27, 28; 3:7, 12, 21). Christ states that he is coming in six of the seven letters (2:5, 16, 25, 3:3, 11, 20), climaxing with v. 3:20: "Listen! I am standing at the door, knocking." The letters are a guided reading through the key moments of the Hebrew Scriptures, showing that they function as a "revelation of Jesus Christ" (1:1). Each one of them closes with a promise of participation in the messianic kingdom. For John, that is the church, symbolized in its fullness by the "seven churches." God's revelation of Jesus Christ has its fulfillment in the historical coming of Jesus Christ, constantly foretold in the ancient Scriptures whose true author, the one like a Son of Man, tells John what the mediating angel must write (see 1:19).

The letters no doubt focus on the lax living of some members of the churches, mainly emerging from the early church's encounter with the Greco-Roman world, but also associated with local tensions between Jews and Christians. Part of that may have been a too easy accommodation of early forms of the emperor cult. But these interpretations are only part of the message of the letters.

The revelation of Jesus Christ has two moments. The revelation found in the story of Israel has been presented in the hearing of the trumpet, and John is instructed to "write in a book what you see and send it to the seven churches" (1:9-11. See v. 11). This "writing" is to announce the coming of Christ as the culmination of Israel's Scriptures. This is "what you see." But the sacred story of Israel prefigures the reality that Christ would bring: the reconciliation of humankind with God and the gift of divine and eternal life (see 2:7, 10-11, 17, 27-28; 3:7, 12, 21). That story is yet to be told. Thus, the second instruction, given to John by the one like a Son of Man is different: "Write what you have seen, what is, and what is to take place after this" (2:20). It points to the fullness of the revelation brought by Jesus Christ, whose death and resurrection gives meaning to the whole of Scripture. That story will be told across the remaining "sevens" that shape the narrative of the book of Revelation.

CHAPTER THREE

# Second Week of Easter: Friday and Saturday

## Making Sense of Revelation 4:1–5:14

Revelation 4:1–8:1 is dedicated to the opening of the seals of a scroll held in the right hand of God (see 5:1) by the slain yet risen Lamb (see 5:6; 6:1, 3, 5, 7, 9, 12; 8:1). The opening of the seven seals and the consequences of the openings for those upon earth are introduced by events that take place "in heaven": "After this I looked, and there in heaven a door stood open" (4:1). The readings for the Friday and Saturday of the Second Week of Easter focus upon two moments in a single "heavenly encounter": the vision of God the lord of creation (Friday: 4:1-11) and the vision of the Son of Man (Saturday: 5:1-14).

### Heavenly encounters (4:1–5:14)

John introduces the next major section of his work by looking back to the heavenly experience that introduced the seven letters, expanding and deepening it. As with 1:9-20, what John sees in 4:1–5:14 is heavenly. There is an aperture between heaven and earth; John is on one side of the door, and heaven is on the other (4:1). John introduces an experience that develops his revelation of Jesus Christ (1:1) across the story of Israel and the Christian church. The sound of the trumpet indicates that, despite the direct vision, the revelation is still mediated (see Exod 19:16). As in 1:10, John is "in the Spirit" (v. 2a). The heavenly vision touches the inner and holiest elements in the visionary. Divine revelation is mediated through human illumination and inspiration. The door opened in heaven signifies the beginning of a revelation of the divine salvific intervention that will take place in two stages: at the creation where it began (4:2b-11), perfected in the universal saving death and resurrection of the Lamb (5:1-17).

John's allusive use of Daniel 7 provides the essential background for these two moments. The lordship of the creator looks back to the presentation of God, the "ancient of days" seated upon his throne in Daniel 7:9-10. The saving presence of the Lamb reimagines the coming of the one like a Son of Man in Daniel 7:13-14, to whom an everlasting dominion is given.

# FRIDAY

## *God and creation (4:1-11)*

After the vision of heaven through the door that stood open, and the summons to "come up," to be shown "what must take place after this" (4:1), John sees the divinity seated upon a throne (v. 2). The word "God" only appears toward the end of this first vision (see vv. 8b, 11a), but the background of Daniel 7:9-10, the use of precious stones to describe him (jasper and carnelian), his being surrounded by a rainbow that also has the appearance of a precious stone (emerald) (v. 3), and the behavior of the heavenly court (vv. 4-5) make it clear that the figure on the throne is divine. The same must be said for the description of the flashes of lightning, rumblings, and peals of thunder that emanate from the throne, indicating the source of their authority (v. 5a). Lightning, rumblings, and peals of thunder are frightening human experiences; but they appear regularly in biblical theophanies (see Exod 29:16; Job 36:30-32;

Ps 77:17-18; Ezek 1:4, 13, 14, 24). This formula, or variations upon it, will reappear elsewhere in Revelation. They have their origin and authority with God.

Throughout the first vision, the divine figure on the throne is the focus of all the attention and action. God is distinct from the "twenty-four elders" who also have thrones, are dressed in white, and have crowns on their heads (v. 4). They are figures of great dignity, but as the scene closes, the audience is told that they *will* fall down, they *will* worship the one on the throne, and they *will* cast their crowns before his throne (v. 10). Many suggestions have been made concerning the identity of these elders, but a definitive solution is beyond us. John communicates that they are very important members of the heavenly court, in close association with the divinity.

The "four living creatures" (vv. 6-7) are associated with the earth: the four elements, the four winds, the four corners of the earth. But John gives them cosmic significance through his use of Ezekiel 1:5-14. There, John has also found the idea of many eyes (v. 8; see Ezek 1:18), a symbol of the ability to see and provide for everything the earth needs. But instead of the *four* wings that the cherubim have in Ezekiel 1:6, John describes them as having *six* wings, associating them with the seraphim of Isaiah 6:2, and subsequently with God's creation. According to Genesis 1:1–2:1, God created and organized the earth in *six* days. Finally, in a further subtle use of Ezekiel, John has *each* of them with a *different* face (v. 7), while in Ezekiel all four faces are possessed by each of the living creatures (Ezek 1:10). For John, the individuality of each living creature must be affirmed, as each will play an individual role in summoning the four horses and their riders as the Lamb opens the first four seals (6:1, 3, 5, 7). The four living creatures, like the twenty-four elders, "give glory and honor and thanks to the one who is seated on the throne" (v. 9).

The twenty-four governors of the heavens and the four living creatures who care for the earth are assembled (vv. 4, 6b-7). They will worship and honor the one seated on the throne (vv. 10-11). In front of the throne there are "seven flaming torches, which are the seven spirits of God" and "something like a sea of glass, like crystal" (vv. 5b-6a). A chain of biblical images generates this passage. In the first place they recall the creative activity of God who made heaven and earth from the void, and the Spirit of God moving over the waters: the crystal-clear waters of God's creation (see Gen 1:1-2). This recalls Isaiah 66:1: "Heaven is my throne and the earth is my footstool." Heaven, earth, and the seas are at the center of the assembly, and the fullness of the Spirit (seven) is also there.[1]

The fundamental message of 4:1-11 is found in the four living creatures' praise and exaltation of God the Almighty's holiness (v. 8b), and the promise of a *future* simultaneous exaltation of God by the twenty-four elders (v. 11). The first stage in John's two-stage heavenly encounter is a heavenly liturgy recognizing and honoring God the creator of all things. His holiness and his almighty and eternal being are affirmed by the four living things (v. 8b). The twenty-four elders recognize the one on the throne as Lord and God, worthy of all glory and honor and power (v. 11a). The reason for this acclaim is provided in the final words of the song of the twenty-four elders: "For you created all things, and by your will they existed and were created" (v. 11b). The lords of the heavens (the twenty-four elders) and the carers of the earth (the four living creatures) will give homage to the creator of all things. They are subject to the Almighty God, who brought all things into existence.

I have insisted that the homage given to God the creator by the four living beings and the twenty-four elders is simultaneous, but it will take place *in the future*. The NRSV translation, following an almost universal interpretation of this

[1] The *Liturgy of the Hours* uses a combination of the following reflections on 4:11; 5:9, 10, 12 as the canticle for Evening Prayer (Evening Prayer II, except when otherwise indicated): the Tuesday of all four weeks, the feasts of the Sacred Heart (Evening Prayer I), Exaltation of the Holy Cross (14 September), All Saints (1 November), Christ the King, and the Common of One and of Several Martyr(s).

passage, associates the actions of the living beings and the elders as follows: "And *whenever* the living creatures give glory . . . the twenty-four elders fall before the one who is seated on the throne . . . and worship" (vv. 9-10). This interpretation indicates that the gesture is repeated over and over again. Every time the four creatures give glory and honor, the twenty-four elders repeat their gestures. This does not do justice to the Greek that uses an indication of time: "when" (*hotan*), followed by verbs in the future tense: "they will give [*dōsousin*] . . . they will fall [*pesousin*] . . . and they will worship [*proskunēsousin*] . . . and they will cast [*balousin*] their crowns" (vv. 9, 10 AT). This must refer to a time in the future when this gesture will take place, once and for all.

John narrates *two stages* of God's saving design. This future oriented moment of total submission on arrival at 4:11 will be clarified as the elders and the living creatures subject themselves, giving honor and praise *to the Lamb* in 5:11-14, the next episode in the narrative. Joined by many angels, the elders and the living creatures "fall down" (5:8) and "worship" (v. 14). The *future* oriented praise and honor (4:9-11) will be given to the creator God only after the slain and risen Lamb, who receives everything from the one seated on the throne, has taken the scroll from his right hand (5:1-8a). Only then the subordination of all powers and authorities to the creator God and the slain yet risen Lamb is complete (vv. 8b-14).

# SATURDAY

*The Lamb and universal salvation (5:1-14)*

The heavenly episodes of 4:1–5:14 form a unified narrative. "There are two separate visions, and two separate events, one following the other but intimately linked."[2] All characters from

---

[2] Corsini, *The Apocalypse*, 132.

4:1-11 reappear in 5:1-14. But a new character, the Lamb, appears for the first time in the story (5:5-6). The other new element in the story is the scroll held in the right hand of the one seated on the throne. The Lamb and the scroll become the focus of 5:1-14 and beyond, as its seals will be opened across 6:1–8:1. The one God, creator and Lord of all (5:1), holds the scroll, written on both sides (see Ezek 2:9-10) in his right hand. But it is sealed. For John, the scroll represents a communication of God's word to humankind, in both the Scriptures of Israel and the gift of life, which passes from God to all humankind through the crucified and risen Lamb. Daniel 7:10 plays its part in the identification of the scroll. There, as the one upon the throne exercises judgment, the scrolls were opened. The scroll communicates between God and humankind. It is the place where those favorably judged will be listed. However, this scroll cannot be read and understood. It is "sealed" against human understanding. A mighty angel from the assembly around the throne cries out: "Who is worthy to open the scroll and break its seals?" (v. 2). The uniqueness of the one who is worthy is highlighted by John's affirmation that *no one* (Greek: *oudeis*) in heaven, on earth, or under the earth—not even the twenty-four elders and the four living creatures—was able to perform that task. The book of life remains closed (v. 3). The situation of an unfulfilled possibility—a book within which the names of the living are inscribed, in the right hand of God, that no one is worthy to open or look into—reduces John to bitter tears (v. 4).

But one of the twenty-four elders, a major figure in the divine hierarchy (see 4:4), comforts John in his tears and introduces the new character (v. 5). The titles used by the elder in his presentation of the one worthy to open the seals are familiar Jewish messianic titles: the Lion of the tribe of Judah, the root of David. The elder promises that the seven seals of the scroll will be opened with the advent of the fulfillment of Jewish hopes. The introduction of the new character is followed by a description of the action that authorizes him to open the seals:

he "has conquered." His Davidic origins and his conquering activity associate him with Jewish messianic hopes. For the Jewish-Christian John, the one who is worthy to conquer by opening the secrets is the fulfillment of Jewish messianic hope. But working within his Jewish-Christian world, he has re-interpreted the messianic "lion" who will conquer, as "the Lamb." The enigma of a crucified and risen Messiah emerges (see 1 Cor 1:21-25).

There is a logical, theological, and Christological link be-tween the Lord and creator God of Israel, the Scriptures of Israel, the slain and risen Lamb as the giver of life, and the Christian community. But the sequence between them is not *historical*. The heavenly visions *transcend* history but make sense of history. The Lamb is the only one worthy of opening the seals. For John, both Israel and the Christian church find their meaning in and through the one worthy to open the seals.

The Lamb appears for the first time, "between the throne and the four living creatures and among the elders" (v. 6a). The uniqueness of the Lamb is already found in the description of his *location*. The vision is in heaven, and his closeness to the one seated on the throne hints at his divine status. Such status will be rendered explicit as the scene unfolds, when the Lamb is honored, side by side with the one seated on the throne (see vv. 13-14). The Lamb is not part of God's creation. They exist from the foundation of the world (see 4:11. See John 1:1). But the elder has introduced the Lamb as one who "has conquered" (v. 5).

The audience is told how the victory took place. The Lamb is "standing [*estēkos*] as if it had been slaughtered [*esphagme-non*]" (v. 6b). The Christian audience identifies this description of the slaughtered yet standing Lamb with belief in the victory of the death and resurrection of Jesus Christ over sin. In this first appearance of the Lamb in the narrative *we are introduced to one of the unique contributions of Revelation to Christian thought*. The one seated on the throne and the slain and risen Lamb belong together in the heavenly and divine realm. As such, the rest of the heavenly world will honor them both (vv. 11-14). The preexistent Lamb, standing before the Almighty God, bears the marks of Jesus Christ, crucified and risen. The saving event of Jesus' death and resurrection transcends human history. The limitations of time, as experienced by creation and its subsequent history, do not apply to the Lamb. From all time the slain and risen Lamb has been part of God's design (see 13:8).

Using the background of Ezekiel 1:18, the Lamb has seven horns, a symbol of the fullness of strength, and the fullness of sight through the seven eyes that see all. Already in the prologue to the book, in 1:1-5 John manifested his awareness of the "trinitarian" aspect of God's intervention (v. 1: God and Jesus Christ; v. 2: God and Jesus Christ; v. 4: God and the Spirit; v. 5: Jesus Christ). This theme returns here, as the gaze of the seven eyes, cast in every direction "are the seven spirits of God sent out into all the earth": the fullness of the presence of the Spirit that emanates from the slain and risen Lamb (5:6c). The figure of the Lamb on his very first appearance is significant. Located "in heaven," outside the constraints of history; slain yet standing between Almighty God and the heavenly court, the Lamb has conquered through his death and resurrection, and the fullness of the Spirit of God reaches out to all the earth (see Ezek 1:19-20).

In v. 7 the Lamb received from God's right hand, the location of all authority.[3] "All that he is and has comes from all time and unto all time, from God, his Father."[4] When the Lamb "received" the scroll from the right hand of God, the four living creatures and the twenty-four elders "fell" before him (v. 8a. See 4:10). These verbs are in the aorist tense, regularly associated with a historical once-and-for-all occurrence. What that occurrence means will be indicated in their song of v. 9.

---

[3] He does not "take" the scroll (as in the NRSV). He "received" (Greek: *elaben*) it.

[4] Corsini, *Apocalypse*, 133.

Each of the four living creatures and the twenty-four elders holds a harp, an instrument that accompanies their song, and golden bowls full of incense. The gold of the bowls indicates that they belong to the divine world, and they contain "the prayers of the saints" (v. 8b). This is the first reference to "the saints" (Greek: *hoi hagioi*). Most interpreters link them, the incense, and their prayers in the golden bowls, with the prayers of the saints of the Christian community that will rise before the Lamb. But the biblical expression "the saints" is very important in Daniel 7 (see vv. 18, 21, 22 [twice], 27. See also Ps 34:10). This use of "the saints" provides essential background to the two stages of the heavenly experience narrated in 4:1–5:14. For Daniel, addressing the faithful during the persecution under Antiochus IV, "the saints" represented loyal Israel experiencing violence and rejection because of their allegiance to the Law and the prophets, and their faithful and patient waiting for the fulfillment of the messianic promises made to Israel (see Dan 7:19-27). In the heavenly vision of Revelation 5:9-13, the living creatures and the elders, holding the prayers of the "saints" of Israel, sing a *new song* (v. 9).[5]

A *new reality* of the divine story is articulated in the hymn. The Lamb is worthy to open the scrolls because his death and resurrection has introduced a new era in God's saving intervention into human history. The blood that flowed from his slaughter has "ransomed for God the saints from every tribe and language and nation" (v. 9bc). While the living creatures and the elders raise the prayers of the saints of Israel, the death and resurrection of Jesus has redeemed saints from all the tribes, from every language, people, and nation. This event made sense of Israel's sacred history, as the saints of the Most High raised their prayers and remained faithful, placing their trust in the messianic promises. But the historical event of the death and resurrection of the slain yet standing Lamb broached

[5] Revelation 5:11-14 provides the second reading in the Liturgy of the Word for the Third Sunday of Easter in Year C.

the Christian era. All are swept into a new relationship with God: a royal priesthood. The promises to the saints of God, from Israel who remained faithful to the Law and the prophets and waited for the fulfillment of Israel's messianic hopes (v. 8), are now available to all humankind because of the death and resurrection of Jesus Christ (v. 9). As the saints of the Most High were promised an everlasting kingdom and submission from all the nations (Dan 7:27), the death and resurrection of Jesus Christ has made possible the reign on earth of a universal royal priesthood serving God (Rev 5:10. See 1:5-6).

What "sealed" the scroll in such a fashion that no one had authority to open it? No one in heaven and on earth was worthy to open the scroll (vv. 3-4). But the seals are broken open by the one who was slaughtered, and whose blood ransomed humankind. From a Christian understanding of God's sacred history, the seals are the result of a long history of sin, from the biblical first sin of disobedience, through a history of sinfulness that has excluded humankind from access to the divine life. Many of the visionary experiences of John will describe this long history of sin. Only the Lamb is worthy to open the seals because of the redemptive effect of his death and resurrection. By means of his sacrifice he ransomed the saints of all times and places for God.

The heavenly introduction to the opening of the seven seals draws to a close. John takes his audience back to the closure of 4:1-11 in the praise and glory to God rendered by the four living creatures and the elders in vv. 9-11. But he expands upon it in 5:11-14. As we saw in our reading of 4:9-11, the *future tense* was used throughout to speak of a future time *when* the heavenly court would give thanks, fall, worship, and cast their crowns before the throne. The introduction of the slain and risen Lamb into the narrative in 5:6 draws that future into the present. The expansion also involves a greater choir than the living beings and the elders. They are joined by "the voice of many angels surrounding the throne" (v. 11a). A sense of universality is communicated by the immensity of the numbers:

"myriads of myriads and thousands of thousands" (v. 11c). In 4:8c only the elders and the living creatures praised God's holiness. In 5:12, along with the angelic hosts, they praise the worthiness of the Lamb, to whom all power and wealth and might and honor and glory and blessing are due (v. 12). As he "received" the scroll from the right hand of God (v. 7), he is deemed worthy "to receive" power and wealth and wisdom and might (v. 12). The focus is squarely upon the exaltation of the Lamb. But this focus is promptly associated with an exaltation of *both* the one seated on the throne *and* the Lamb (v. 13).

The expansion of the heavenly creatures singing the praises of the Lamb in vv. 11-12 through the association of the innumerable number of angels from around the throne is further developed in vv. 13-14. The initial vision of the one seated on the throne in the first stage, before the Lamb appeared (4:1-11), was accompanied by the governors of the heavenly spheres, the twenty-four elders, and those whose task is to care for the earth, the four living creatures (see 4:4, 6), along with the image of God's creation as "the sea of glass like crystal" (v. 6). In the second stage, after the Lamb has appeared before the one seated on the throne, these representative images are transformed and universalized. As a result of the appearance of the slain and risen Lamb, all that has been represented in 4:4-6 enters the narrative in an expanded form to praise God and the Lamb in 5:13-14: "[E]very creature in heaven and on earth and under the earth and in the sea" (5:13) sings a blessing to honor and glorify *both* the one seated on the throne *and* the Lamb (v. 13b).

There is only one revelation of Jesus Christ, but it takes place across two stages. In the first place it is available in the revelation of God as Lord and Creator found in the sacred story of Israel (4:1-11). The death and resurrection of Jesus broaches a new era where the saving effects of the blood of the Lamb opens the long-awaited universal possibility of divine life (5:1-14). One leads to the other, and each one makes sense because of the other. In unconditional agreement, the elders prostrate themselves and worship (v. 14). The divine one on the throne and the divine slain and risen Lamb who surpasses and transcends Daniel's one like the Son of Man are to be blessed, honored and glorified forever (v. 13): "Amen!" (v. 14).

# CHAPTER FOUR

# *Third Week of Easter: Sunday and Monday*

## Making Sense of Revelation 6:1–8:1

The *Liturgy of the Hours* reflects upon the opening of the first five seals on the Sunday of the Third Week of Easter. The first part (6:12-17) of the visions accompanying the opening of the sixth seal also appears in the Sunday reading. The remaining visions that accompany the opening of the sixth seal (7:1-17) appear in the reading for Monday.[1]

The Lamb opens the seals, one by one. The seven seals are opened in a pattern of 4 + 3. The four living creatures order: "Come!" Four horses and their riders appear, each one bringing consequences. The use of horses is an allusion to the colored horses of Zechariah 1:8 and 6:2-8, symbols of God's patrolling of the four empires at the four corners of the earth. The white, red, and black colors appear in Zechariah, but only John has a "greenish" horse. The imagery of the horses and their riders summoned in the first four seals is generated by a series of allusions to Genesis 1–5. The opening of the final three

---

[1] The *Liturgy of the Hours* offers Revelation 7:1-17 for the reading of the Monday of the Third Week. For our purposes, 8:1 (opening the reading for Tuesday in the *Liturgy of the Hours*) will be included. The seventh seal is opened, and silence descends.

seals (6:9–8:1) makes known the saving effects of the death and resurrection of Jesus Christ.

# SUNDAY

### *The first seal: White horse and rider—humankind's potential (6:1-2)*

The Lamb opens the first seal, the living creature summons with the voice of thunder, and John sees a white horse (6:1). A rider carrying a bow is saddled on the white horse. He is given a crown. He comes out conquering, so that he will conquer. Positive elements appear in the presentation of first horse and its rider. The following horses and riders bring violence and suffering. To this point, only heavenly beings have been described as wearing crowns (4:2, 10). The image of a horse and a rider, however, belongs to the human sphere, and the crown "was given to him" (6:2). It is not something that the rider has by right, as with the heavenly twenty-four elders. Adding to this optimism is the indication that the rider of the white horse came out "conquering" and "so that he will conquer" (v. 2 AT).

The opening of the seals begins with an allegory on the potential of humankind, created in the image of God (Gen 1:26-27), lord of creation and friend of God (2:4b-24). According to the biblical story, man and woman were created perfect, in a privileged relationship with God, whose image they were (Gen 1:26-27). Thus, the coming of the white horse and its rider is an allegory of the *possibilities* of the human condition. He came "conquering." But the rider carries a bow, an instrument that can bring about good or evil. The bow, like the sword, is used as a symbol of God's punitive action (see Isa 41:2), but also in descriptions of people who play a role in God's design, as the Medes destroy Babylon with the bow (Jer 50: 14, 29, 42; 51:3), a gift of God to Hagar, so that he might become a great nation (Gen 21:17-21). But ultimate trust must be in the Lord, not in the bow or the sword (Ps 44:6).

A choice must be made: the Lord or the bow? Adam and Eve had a choice (Gen 2:15-17). The audience knows that man and woman failed as they made their choice against the expressed will of the one who made them and they suffered subsequent punishment (Gen 3:1-24). Whatever that choice may have been, the promise is made that the rider of the white horse comes so that he will conquer (v. 2). In a story of failure, Israel's Scripture promises that false choices are not the end of God's relationship with humankind (see Gen 3:15). The possibilities of humankind will not be thwarted by human failure. He came out, "so that he will conquer" (v. 2 AT). Human *potential* still belongs to the story of women and men.

### The second seal:
### Bright red horse and rider—violence (6:3-4)

The second living creature calls out "Come!" and a bright red horse appears, a color traditionally associated with war and violence (v. 3). The rider of the horse is given a great sword and is "permitted to take peace from the earth" (v. 4). Peace will be taken away by human beings slaying one another with "a great sword," the traditional instrument for killing and execution. Significantly, the very first recorded action of the children of Adam and Eve, Cain and Abel, is Cain's slaying of Abel (Gen 4:1-16). The sufferings of warfare expand from these beginnings. In contrast to the peace and order that characterized God's creative activity (Gen 1:1–2:24), human sin (Gen 3:1-25), and warfare and its bloody consequences follow, after the violent slaying of Abel (Gen 4:1-12).

### The third seal: Black horse and rider—toil (6:5-6)

The coming of a black horse and its rider, summoned by the living creature, appears holding a measuring scale (v. 5). A voice comes from the four living beings saying that there will be a lack of essential foods: bread, wine, and oil. Association with the Genesis story provides a key to its interpretation. Humankind no longer enjoys the limitless fruits of the garden (Gen 2:8-9, 15-16), as the result of the Fall. Animals rebel, plants of the earth and the earth itself rebels (Gen 3:14-19): "By the sweat of your face you shall eat bread" (Gen 3:19). The Genesis narrative, a profound mythical explanation of the common and universal experience of the struggle to produce and provide sufficient food, addresses a human situation that persists to this day.

## The fourth seal:
## Pallid green horse and rider—death (6:7-8a)

The name of the fourth rider is death, and Hades followed with him (v. 8a). John describes the color, in Greek, as *chlōros*. Literally, this means "green." While in real life a white, red, and black horse are possible, there is no such thing as a green horse. The colors, therefore, communicate more than a visible color. From antiquity, the color of the final horse has long been associated with the color of death. The translation "greenish" associates the color of the horse with the color of death, seen in the color of a dead body. This interpretation points to the most serious of all consequences of humankind's sinfulness: death as the result of human disobedience (Gen 3:19; Rom 5:12).

But the association of "death, and Hades followed with him" with the name of the rider, indicates more than the universal reality of physical death that, according to the Bible, is the result of sin. From well before biblical times, Greek and Roman traditions spoke of "Hades" as the dwelling place of the dead.[2] It equates to the biblical use of "Sheol." John's placing them side by side, one as the consequence of the other, indicates that they belong together: death and Hades form the same double reality. This is the way John presented them in his prologue, when told by the one like a Son of Man that he

---

[2] See Richard Bauckham, "Hades" in David Noel Freedman, ed., *The Anchor Bible Dictionary*, 6 vols. (New York: Doubleday, 1992), 3:14-15.

had the keys "of Death and Hades" (2:17 AT). The fall from privilege (6:1-2) into sinfulness has led to the reality of a double death: physical death (Death) and being cast into a place where there is no presence of God (Hades). The loss of original blessedness has produced physical and spiritual death for humankind.

## A concluding summary (6:8b)

A traditional interpretation of the Greek text, into which punctuation has been inserted over the centuries, is represented by the NRSV translation of v. 8. It links v. 8b with v. 8a: "Its rider's name was Death, and Hades followed with him; they were given authority over a fourth of the earth." It is possible that a stronger break should come between the description of the rider in v. 8a and the gift of authority in v. 8b. A literal translation of the Greek text of v. 8b states: "And authority was given to them." The "them" looks back to all four horses and riders: "And to them was given authority over one fourth of the earth" (v. 8b). In this interpretation, v. 8b serves as a statement that concludes the presentation of the opening of the first four seals. It describes the gift of authority to the four horses and their riders, associating what has been described in 6:1-8a with the ancient theme of the four world empires. The four horses and the four riders are the empires who are given authority over a quarter of the earth as a result of sin. Only partial control is granted. Only God and the Lamb have universal lordship, no matter how damaging the empires might be. What was said of the second and the third horse takes place because they exercise their authority: to kill (v. 4) with famine, pestilence, and wild beasts (v. 6), traditional dangers to human beings. The "wild beasts [Greek: *tōn thēriōn*] of the earth" may be linked with the emergence of wild beasts in Genesis 3:14, a consequence of the Fall: "Cursed are you among all animals and among all wild creatures."

The opening of the first four seals is an allegory of humankind's fall from original blessing. God is the active agent. The

Lamb has opened the seals; the crown "was given" to the first rider (v. 2); the second rider "was permitted" to take away peace, as a great sword "was given" (v. 4); the four creatures tell of the lack of food (v. 6). To the four horses and their riders "authority was given" (v. 8b). The four empires exist as a result of human sinfulness, and their authority spreads sin and violence across the face of the earth. However, the process of sin and consequent punishment, meted out by the misuse of the authority of the four empires, is part of God's design. God "permits" such atrocities which originate in the disobedience of man and woman. The Lamb opened the seals that unleashed the horsemen, and God has "permitted" suffering and death. Its roots lie in human sin and disobedience. Its resolution lies with God and the Lamb, the Alpha and the Omega, the first and the last, the beginning and end of all human history (see 1:8, 17; 2:8; 21:6; 22:13).

For John, the four empires indicate *all empires*. This includes the Roman Empire that, for John, was the last of the empires, somewhat like the rule of Antiochus IV that concluded the cycle of the four beasts from the sea (Dan 7:1-11). What is described in the opening of the first four seals is not the end of the story. In Daniel 7:1-14, the messianic victory takes place in the one like the Son of Man, as the empires have their power taken from them, or are destroyed. Similarly, but in a way that transcends the authority given to Daniel's one like a Son of Man, for John all authority is given to the slain yet risen Lamb (5:6. See 1:12-17).

## Opening the final three seals (6:9–8:1)

### The fifth seal:
### Saints of Israel, waiting under the altar (6:9-11)

When the Lamb opens the fifth seal, John sees the souls of those "who had been slaughtered for the word of God and for the witness they had borne" (AT). Their souls are located "under the altar" (v. 9). They ask God: "Sovereign Lord, holy and true, how long will it be before you judge and avenge our blood on the inhabitants of the earth?" (v. 10). The passage envisions an in-between-time between the "now" and the "little longer" (see v. 11b). But the blessings that flow from the definitive victory of God over sin are already given to them as they rest under the altar. They were each *given a white robe*. The audience accepts that these slain souls enjoy the gift of divine life through this gift of the white robe, *before the numbers of their fellow servants are complete* (v. 11). God tells them "to rest a little longer" (v. 11). Their being slain for the word of God and for bearing witness (v. 9) is not the end of a divinely designed process. The number of those to be caught up in this process is not yet complete. More time must pass. But John sees witnesses who already participate in divine life and wait under the altar. They belong to a "past," and are waiting for the final event that will make sense of that past. They are all those "saints" of Israel who had lived by the Law (the word of God), and who had maintained their faith in the messianic promises of the prophets (the witness they had borne).

Their reception of the white robe (v. 11) gives them access to the divine life made possible by the slain and risen Lamb, even though their witness and death took place across the period of Israel's sacred history. These martyrs are not part of the sacrifices made on the altar of Jerusalem in Israel's liturgies. They are waiting "under the altar" in this heavenly vision. They will eventually form part of a new liturgy offered to God. But this is not possible until the full assembly of all those whom the blood of the slaughtered Lamb "ransomed for God saints from every tribe and language and people and nation." (5:9). Only then will God have generated "a kingdom [of] priests serving our God" (5:10). God's final victory will produce priests serving God in an endless liturgy (see 1:5-6).

Returning to foundational themes stated during the heavenly events that introduced the opening of the seals (4:1–5:14), the opening of the fifth seal carries the narrative further. The first four seals told of the fall of humankind through disobedience, and the subsequent violence and sin (6:1-8). Across the period of Israel, suffering these atrocities, some remained faithful to God in their obedience to the Torah ("the word of God"), and their loyal expectation of the Messiah, announced by the prophets ("for the testimony they had given"). Even though the final victory of God in the death and resurrection of Jesus Christ has not yet taken place in history, each one of them is already *given* a white robe (v. 11). The theme of the perennial availability of the saving effects of the death and resurrection of Jesus comes into play here. These martyrs have access to the divine life, *before* the historical events of Jesus' crucifixion and resurrection (v. 11), because those saving mysteries have been available from the beginning of time (see 5:6; 13:8). They have a share in the slaying of the Lamb before the foundation of the world. They are thus *given* the white robe. The slain and risen Lamb is unveiling this story. He is the crucial agent in the opening of the seals; he alone is worthy of this sacred role (see 5:4, 9).

Israel's saints are not told to wait till the eschatological end of all time for Jesus' second coming, but for the time of the death and resurrection of Jesus Christ. That event will conclude and give meaning to the sacred history of Israel, setting in motion a new era. There will be a final coming (see 22:20), but the victory of God has already been won in the death and resurrection of his Son. To the members of a believing Christian community, as we will see, the white garment is already given. There is a time *before* the death and resurrection of Jesus when the saints are *given* the white garment (6:11), and a time *after* it when believers from every nation, tribe, people and tongue are "robed in white" (7:9).

A further detail in v. 11 calls for attention. The souls of the slain in Israel are told to rest a little longer so that the number would be complete. But there are two groups in that complete number indicated by the Greek "and . . . and." The voice tells them that they are to rest "until the number would be complete *both* of their fellow servants *and* of their brothers and sisters, who were soon to be killed as they themselves had been killed." It is not only those who are yet to be killed that will complete the number, but also the "fellow servants" of those slain in Israel. The saving effects of the death and resurrection, the possession of the white robe, cannot be limited to martyrs. There are many other witnesses who will form part of the completion of that number, made possible by the death and resurrection of Jesus: fellow servants.

### *The sixth seal: The cosmic effects of the death of the Lamb (Part One: 6:12-17)*

The extent of consequences of the Lamb's opening of the sixth seal is more complex and takes longer to narrate than those of the first five seals (6:12–7:17). The opening of the sixth seal produces a long sequence of visions that the audience associates with descriptions of the eschatological end of all things, in biblical and Jewish tradition (6:12-17). That time will be marked by a great earthquake (e.g. Ezek 38:19), the blackening of the sun (e.g. Isa 50:3; Joel 3:14-15), the falling of the stars of the sky (Isa 13:9-10; Ezek 32:7-8; Joel 2:10), the rolling up of the sky like a scroll and the shaking of the islands and mountains (e.g. Isa 34:4; Ezek 26:18), the humiliation of all, from the leaders and the powerful to the free and the slaves (e.g. Isa 2:9-11, 19-21; 24:21-22; 34:12; Ezek 26:15-17; Zeph 1:14-18), hiding in the caves and rocks of the mountains, pleading with the Lord to cover and hide them from the coming wrath (Hos 10:8). For John this is not the wrath of God's final intervention, but the "wrath of the Lamb" (Rev 6:16). The slain yet standing Lamb (5:6) will execute judgment, and everyone, from kings to slaves, will wonder "who is able to stand?" (v. 17).

# MONDAY

### *The sixth seal: The cosmic effects of the death of the Lamb (Part Two: 7:1-17)*

The expected response to this question is: "No one." But such is not the case. The events that continue the narrative accompanying the opening of the sixth seal provide a positive answer to the provocative question of v. 17. Four angels "standing" (7:1) sign "the servants of our God": the 144,000 sealed with the seal of the living God (7:1-8). Then there are others who stand before the throne and the Lamb (7:9): the multitude who are products of the great ordeal, whose robes have been washed white in the blood of the Lamb (7:9-17).

John communicates a vision that marks a decisive time in God's plan, the inevitable judgment exercised by the slain and risen Lamb. Who can be saved from the wrath of the Lamb in this "great day" (vv. 16-17)? The response to this question, framed in a two-phased presentation of those who are saved from the wrath of the Lamb indicates that 6:12-17 is not about the end of all time. Closely related by the expression "after this" in 7:1, followed by "after these things" in v. 9, the opening of the sixth seal brings the announcement of "times," in a temporal sequence. Three moments are narrated: [1] judgment, and a question asking who can be saved (6:12-17), [2] the vision of the 144,000 (7:1-8), and [3] the vision of those who have come out of the great tribulation, and wear garments washed white in the blood of the Lamb (7:9-17).

Flowing from the announcement of the "wrath [that] has come" (6:12-17), vv. 9-17 address the judgment of an immense number of those "who have come out of the great ordeal," whose robes have been made white by the blood of the Lamb (see vv. 9, 14). The active agents in vv. 1-9 are angels (vv. 1-3). An angel ascending from the rising sun has the seal of the living God (v. 2). This angel prohibits the four angels that stand at the corners of the earth from damaging creation, "until we have marked the servants of our God with a seal on their foreheads" (v. 3). The design of God is *mediated* through an angel. This is a sign that those saved in vv. 7-8 belong to Israel's sacred history. On the other hand, in vv. 9-17, those standing before the Lamb (v. 9) are described as having come out of the great tribulation with garments washed white in the blood of the Lamb (v. 14). These are the saints of the post-Christ era.

The four angels that control the earth (v. 1) remind the audience of the four living creatures before the throne, each possessing six wings, and full of eyes (5:6-8). They are commanded by another angel, one ascending from the rising of the sun, possessing the seal of the living God (7:2). This angel called authoritatively ("with a loud voice") to the four angels, prohibiting them from destroying anything on earth *until* they have marked the foreheads of the servants of God with his seal (v. 3). As the souls of those who had been slaughtered, described in the fifth seal were given a time *until* the number would be complete (6:11), so also those signed by God's seal have their experience *before* an event that is yet to take place. The servants of the fifth seal (9, 11), and the servants of the first group described in the sixth seal are the same (7:3): the saints from Israel's sacred history. The 144,000 made up of 12,000 from each "tribe of the people of Israel" (vv. 4-8) forms a large but *limited* number. Not everyone in Israel is marked with the seal of God by his angel. Nevertheless, there are many from Israel, even if a reduced number, who have been sealed. They will be saved from the effects of the coming judgment, thanks to God's intervention, through his angel. The servants of both the fifth and the sixth seal are "those who had been slaughtered for the word of God and the testimony they had borne" (6:9 AT), Israel's saints who have remained faithful to God's laws, and who had maintained faith in the messianic promises of the prophets.

The immense numbers and the universal nature of the final vision of the sixth seal reaches beyond the saints of Israel. They are not saved by the intervention of an angel, but stand "before the throne, and before the Lamb." They are dressed in white and carry the well-known image of palm branches of victory in their hands (v. 9). Repeating the universal praise of both God and the Lamb of 5:13-14, they indicate that "salvation" belongs to God and the Lamb (v. 10). The attendants of God in the heavenly court of 4:1-11 remain in their places around the throne, repeating their praise of God (7:11-12. See 4:8-11). However, in 4:8-11 the heavenly court looked forward to a time when the living creatures would give praise (v. 9) to the one seated on the throne. They would fall (v. 10) and they would worship (v. 10) and the twenty-four elders would cast their crowns before the throne (v. 11). The time has come, as the saints of the post-Christ era sing praise to the God seated on the throne, and to the Lamb (7:9-10). Thus, they "fell" on their faces and "worshipped" God (v. 11). Even though the court sings only in praise of God (v. 12), the association of God with the Lamb (vv. 9-10) opens a new era, indicated by the past tenses of v. 11. What was once a promise (4:9-11) is now taking place (7:11-12).

This leads one of the elders from the heavenly court to ask John what has generated this: "Who are these robed in white?" Important as the answer to that question might be, the critical element in the elder's question is "where have they come from?" (v. 13). The elder from the court of heaven explains: they have come through "the great tribulation." They have been produced "from/out of" (Greek: *ek*) the great tribulation. They are the fruits of the great tribulation. The whiteness of their robes comes from their participation in the saving blood of the Lamb (v. 14). The great tribulation that has produced this great multitude of all races and nations is the death of Jesus, the slaughtering of the Lamb. The slaughtered Lamb generates the blood that washes white the clothes born by those who emerge from the great tribulation of Jesus Christ's crucifixion.

In a long and unbroken sentence, the elder associates God and the Lamb. "For this reason," the elder explains, they are now in a situation where they can worship before the throne of God, who protects them from all suffering and danger, day and night (vv. 15-16) "because" the Lamb at the center of the throne will be their shepherd and will "guide them to springs of the water of life" (v. 17). The blood of the Lamb has introduced them into the perennial presence of God, who will "wipe away every tear from their eyes" (v. 17). The judgment that has come upon humankind (6:12-17) takes place *because of* the death of Jesus Christ, the pouring out of the blood of the Lamb (7:14). Many will perish (see 6:15-17; 7:2-3). But there are some from the period of Israel's sacred story to whom salvation will be given. Their participation in the death and resurrection of Jesus will be applied to them through the mediation of an angel, who seals them with the seal of God as, like the servants under the altar after the opening of the fifth seal, they wait (7:1-8). The saving reality of Jesus' redeeming blood is applied directly to a great multitude from every nation, tribe, people, and language (vv. 9-17).

*The seventh seal:*
*Silence in heaven greets the victory of the Lamb (8:1)*

The account of the opening of the seventh seal and its consequences is the briefest of all the "sevens," made up of only fourteen Greek words. The opening of the final seal produces "silence in heaven for about half an hour" (8:1). The silence takes place "in heaven." John continues to "bend the genre" in the light of early Christian interpretation of the death and resurrection of Jesus. A solution to the significance of the period of silence lies in the *narrative* of 4:1–8:1. The silence in heaven of 8:1 concludes a series of spectacular visions of worship and acclamation of the one seated on the throne, God, and the Lamb. They all took place "in heaven" (see 4:1), including John's description of the consequences of the opening of the sixth seal: the saving death of Jesus Christ.

*But heavenly liturgy ceases entirely when the seventh seal is opened* (8:1). Silence reigns in heaven as the universal liturgy ceases, in recognition of the saving action of God in and through the death of the Lamb. The silence (8:1) that follows the proclamation of the death of the Lamb (7:9-14) originates in traditional Christian background. In all Synoptic Gospels, the death of Jesus is marked by a period of silence (see Mark 15:38; Matt 27:51; Luke 23:45). Once that association is made, another common element between the Synoptic tradition and Revelation can be traced: the end of the effectiveness of the Jewish cult. The tearing open of the temple veil, and the availability of the holy of holies to all nations who might wish to gaze upon it (Mark 15:38; Matt 27:51; Luke 23:45) means different things for Mark, Matthew, and Luke. But a basic theme is common to each of them: with the death of Jesus, the way to God is no longer limited to Israel, and only through the temple and its practices. That era in God's relationship to humankind, and humankind's relationship with God, has come to an end (see also Mark 11:12-25).[3]

The death of Jesus is followed by a brief period between the death and the resurrection of Jesus, when everything on earth and in heaven, so active and vocal from the opening liturgy (4:1–5:14), and again at the opening of the sixth seal (6:12–7:17), falls silent. For John, that brief period is half an hour.

The silence establishes a definitive break with the Jewish liturgical access to God. But as one period of God's intervention in the human story comes to an end (7:1-8), another begins (7:9-17). A new era, founded on the death and resurrection of Jesus, is about to be set in motion. A brief silence reigns. Each of the "sevens" will close with a description of the effects of the death and resurrection of Jesus. The fourteen words of 8:1 that mark the opening of the seventh seal are the most obscure. They will be clarified as the sixth (10:7: "The mystery of God will be fulfilled") and the seventh trumpet is blown (11:15: "The kingdom of the world has become the kingdom of our Lord and of his Messiah"), and the seventh bowl is poured out (16:17: "It is done!"). John returns again and again to the theme of Jesus' death and resurrection, developing it as his book unfolds, especially at the "seventh" of the letters, seals, trumpets, and bowls.

Although much later, an unknown author from the fourth or fifth century may have caught what was present in the

---

[3] See Francis J. Moloney, *The Gospel of Mark. A Commentary* (Grand Rapids, MI: Baker Academic, 2012), 221–28, for an interpretation of this passage as a narrative symbolizing the end of Jewish cult and the establishment of a new way to God.

thought and practice of early Christianity (see Mark 15:38; Matt 27:51; Luke 23:45). On the Saturday that separates the death of Jesus (Friday) and his resurrection (Sunday), the author proclaimed:

> There is a great silence on earth today, a great silence and stillness. The whole earth keeps silence because the King is asleep. The earth trembled and is still because God has fallen asleep in the flesh and he has raised up all who have slept ever since the world began. (*From an Ancient Homily for Holy Saturday*)[4]

---

[4] The author of this homily is unknown. For the Greek text and a Latin translation of the homily, see PG 43.439–464, where the risen Christ's descent to lead Adam and Eve to glory is a major theme. For the passage cited, see PG 43.439–440. (PG = *Patrologia cursus completus: Series graeca*, ed. J.-P. Migne, 217 vols. [Paris, 1857–1886].) The choice of the cover design for this book, the icon of the risen Christ raising Adam and Eve in the "silence" of Holy Saturday, is closely associated with this early Christian tradition.

# CHAPTER FIVE

# Third Week of Easter:
# Tuesday through Saturday

## Making Sense of Revelation 8:2–11:19

The blowing of the seven trumpets dominates the Third Week of Easter. Tuesday is dedicated to John's report of an initial heavenly encounter and the blowing of the first four trumpets (Rev 8:2-13). Wednesday, Thursday, Friday, and Saturday focus upon the more extended fifth trumpet, the first "woe" (9:1-12); the sixth trumpet, the second "woe" (9:13-21); and the seventh trumpet, the third "woe" (10:1-11 and 11:1-19).

The blowing of trumpets is a feature of the gift of the Law on Sinai (see Exod 19:13, 16, 19; 20:18). It remains central for Israel's praise of God (see, for example, Ps 47:5-7; 98:4-6; 150:3-5); for summoning the people to the celebration of the great feasts that recall God's actions (see, for example, Lev 23:24 [Passover]; 25:9 [Atonement]; Sir 50:16; Ps 81:3); gathering and warning the people in time of difficulty and war (see, for example, Num 10:1-7; 31:6 ; see also 1 Cor 14:8); spectacularly present at the conquering of Jericho, the gateway to the Promised Land (Num 10:1-17). The author of the letter to the Hebrews describes the Old Covenant, now perfected by the mediation of "Jesus, the mediator of the new covenant," as a time in the past when Israel sought "the sound of a trumpet"

(Heb 12:18-24. See vv. 19, 23). Although the sound of a trumpet is associated with the final coming of Jesus (see Matt 24:31; 1 Cor 15:52; 1 Thess 4:16), it is overwhelmingly associated with the Old Covenant. The choice of "trumpets," therefore, is a preliminary hint to the audience that what is about to follow will be concerned with God's revelation in Israel, leading to its consummation in Jesus Christ.

# TUESDAY

### *Heavenly encounters (8:2-6)*

The liturgy in heaven that John witnesses initially focuses upon seven angels "who stand before God" (v. 2). It is not necessary to identify the number "seven" with a particular group of angels, over against all the other angels. The number indicates totality, as the seven churches represented the church as such (1:9–3:22), seven stars in the hand of the Son of Man (1:15, 20; 2:1); the seven spirits represented the universal presence of the spirit (5:6); and the seven candelabra stood for Jewish cult (1:20). Members of the angelic host are before God, subordinate and loyal to God. "Seven trumpets were given to them" by God. But the angels remain inactive until 8:6.

Another angel enters the scene to conduct a liturgy that recalls sacrifice to God, offered at the altar of incense in the Jewish cultic system. However, it takes place in heaven, and thus is the perfect model of what should take place on earth. To this angel God gives a great deal of incense that is to be offered, along with the prayers of "the saints." The altar is described as "golden," part of the divine design and a perfect model of the altar of incense within the Jewish cultic tradition (see Exod 30:1-9; 37:25-28; 1 Kgs 8:64; 9:25). The angel is an agent in God's activity in heaven, but the prayers of "the saints" offered before the throne come from earth. The function of the angel performing this liturgy is to act as an intermediary between earth and heaven, raising incense and the prayers of "the saints" to God (vv. 3-4). The cult of Israel, in which "the saints" turned in prayer to God, needed a mediator to carry the cultic activity of "the saints" to God. John portrays a heavenly Jewish cult, raising incense and the prayers of "the saints" to God (vv. 2-4).

The activity of the angel changes. He ends his liturgical actions as he takes fire, fills the censer with it, and casts it down upon earth. An essential element in the cultic activity, the censer filled with fire, is cast down to earth. "Peals of thunder, rumblings, flashes of lightning, and an earthquake" follow the action (v. 5). The tranquil ritual of a heavenly presentation of incense and prayers rising to God in the Jewish cult (vv. 2-4) is brusquely interrupted by what could be understood, at first sight, as a violent end to the cult and its consequences (v. 5).

This final scene of the heavenly encounter recalls the Synoptic Gospels—especially the Gospel of Matthew—that report the death and resurrection of Jesus accompanied with the same effects (Mark 15:33-39; Matt 27:45-54; 28:1-4; Luke 23:44-45). Jesus' death is greeted with rumblings (Matt 27:51), flashes of lightning (Matt 28:3), and an earthquake (Matt 27:54; 28:2). The conclusion to the heavenly representation of the Jewish cult is the death of Jesus, not the promise of destructive plagues. In a passage common to Luke and Matthew, a prediction from John the Baptist clarifies the association between Jesus' coming judgment and fire: "He will baptize you with the Holy Spirit and fire. His winnowing fork is in his hand, to clear his threshing floor and to gather the wheat into his granary, but the chaff will burn with unquenchable fire" (Luke 3:16b-18; Matt 3:11b-12). The same association is made between the presence of Jesus and the fire of a judgment that causes division is found in Luke 12:49 (see vv. 49-53): "I came to bring fire to the earth, and how I wish it were already kindled!" The death and resurrection of Jesus will bring a fire that judges: some will be condemned and others will be saved. This is the "fire from the altar," thrown down upon the earth (Rev 8:5). The liturgy closes as the angels who have the seven trumpets make ready to blow them (v. 6).

## Blowing the first four trumpets (8:7-13)

### The first trumpet: Burning a third of the sea (8:7)

John indicates the movement from above to below as being "hurled" to the earth. The first description of what was hurled onto the earth is vague: "hail and fire, mixed with blood." The blowing of the trumpet initiates the hurling down of fiery bodies from on high to below. John uses images and experiences that led to the exodus. Thunder, hail, and fire fall upon Egypt when Moses stretches out his hand to heaven. As in Egypt, although without John's proportion of "a third," the hurling down of this first fiery heavenly body burns up a third of the trees and the green grass (see Exod 9:22-35). The fact that each punishment destroys only a third of creation means that not everything is lost!

### The second trumpet: Poisoning a third of the sea (8:8-9)

At the blowing of the second trumpet, the object hurled down from heaven to earth is more explicit: a fiery mountain is thrown down into the sea. The result of this descent, as with the result of the blowing of the first trumpet, recalls the second plague in Egypt that led to the exodus: the waters turn into blood (see Exod 7:17-25). A third of the living creatures die, and a third of the commercial life that uses the sea is destroyed.

### The third trumpet:
### Poisoning a third of the springs (8:10-11)

The fall from heaven of a great star, "blazing like a torch," takes the reader closer to an identification of what is represented by the various descriptions of those "thrown down" or "fallen" from heaven to earth. The great fiery star falls onto a third of the rivers and the springs of water.

The star falling from heaven is given a name, "Wormwood," rendering the waters like its own bitter self. Many die from its bitterness (8:11). This is the only time that the destruction of humans is explicitly mentioned, although they necessarily suffer from the consequences of the fall from heaven of what we can now recognize as the first two angels. However, John's focus is not upon humankind as such. John recalls events from the exodus experience, Israel's experience of the "bitter waters" (Exod 15:22-25. See also Jer 9:15; 23:15). These experiences may bear a sign of hope.

## The fourth trumpet:
## Destruction of a third of the earth's light (8:12-13)

No damaging agent emerges from the blowing of the fourth trumpet. Nothing is cast down, or falls, from heaven to earth. The action that generates the consequences of the blowing of the trumpet is different. Something "strikes" the lights of the earth. The infliction of damage that results from the blowing of the fourth trumpet is the result of the destruction and death that has struck a third of God's creation across the first three trumpets, as the angels were cast down, and fell from heaven to earth. All the light-bearing elements in creation lose a third of their light: the sun, the moon, and the stars. The illumination of the day (the sun) and the night (the moon and the stars) decreases by a third. They no longer perform the task for which they were created by God. This is what it means to be "fallen."

The blowing of the first four trumpets has led to a statement and restatement of the falling of the angels from heaven, and the damage that this generates across God's creation, including humankind. The consequences of the blowing of the first four trumpets are upon God's creation. The angels themselves belong to that creation, but God has thrown them down, cast them out, and they have fallen. Fallen angels are cast down from heaven to earth, but only one-third is destroyed, or ceases to be what it should be (the lights of creation). Nevertheless, hints of a future liberation exist in the repeated allusions to themes from the exodus. God's presence in failure led to freedom.

Closing his account of the blowing of the first four trumpets, John tells of "an eagle crying with a loud voice" in mid-heaven. At first glance, an eagle may appear to add to the threat of the three "woes." However, John again flirts imaginatively with a symbol found throughout the Bible of God's strong and loving care for his people (see, for example, Exod 19:4; Deut 32:11; 2 Sam 1:23; Ps 103:1-5; Ezek 1:10; 10:14; 17:3, 7), coupled with passages that indicate his displeasure (see, for example, Job 9:26; Hos 8:1; Mic 1:16; Dan 4:31). For this context, the association of the eagle with the exodus (Exod 19:4; Deut 32:11) continues to promise hope in the midst of punishment. The cry of the eagle in mid-heaven leads the reader/listener into the theme that unifies the blowing of the final three trumpets: the three "woes" that will fall upon "the inhabitants of the earth" (v. 13).

John continues to tell the biblical saga. Angels fell (see Gen 6:1-4), bringing with their fall the punishments that can be seen and experienced in the ambiguities of Israel's sacred history. However, there is hope, as that history was not an end unto itself. It contained within itself the promise of a future liberation.

## *Blowing the final three trumpets: The three "woes" (9:1–11:19)*

The blowing of the fifth, sixth, and seventh trumpets bring on the three "woes." Unlike the four trumpets that told of the fall of the angels, the "woes" impact upon the human situation. As with the sixth seal, the sixth trumpet, the second "woe," brings more extensive consequences. They are the consequences of the fall of humankind reported in the first "woe," some tragic, and others the bearers of hope: war (9:13-21), the initial saving intervention of God in Israel's sacred history (10:1-11), with its temple and witnesses (11:1-14), pointing forward to the blowing of the seventh trumpet, and the fulfillment of "the mystery of God" (10:7).

# WEDNESDAY

*The first "woe": The fall of humankind (9:1-12)*

At the blowing of the fifth trumpet, a link is made with the portrait of Satan as "the great star falling from heaven" at the blowing of the third trumpet (see v. 1). Satan is given the keys to the abyss: "the shaft of the bottomless pit" (9:1). The audience recalls that in Patmos John had a vision of Jesus Christ who told him: "I am the first and the last, and the living one. I was dead, and see, I am alive forever and ever; and I have the keys of Death and Hades" (1:17b-18). The "time" of the narrative of 9:1 must *precede* the "time" of the narrative of 1:17b-18. Jesus has the keys of death and Hades because he was dead and now he is alive. However, Satan received the keys of the bottomless pit when he fell from heaven (9:1). John is reflecting on prehistory: the origins of the suffering and disorder that have marked the human story from all time. The audience senses that there must have been an event at which the keys were taken from Satan. The one like a Son of Man has said to the church in Philadelphia: "These are the words of the holy one, the true one, who has the key of David, who opens and no one will shut, who shuts and no one opens" (3:7). Toward the end of the narrative, Satan will be bound and locked into the bottomless pit by "an angel coming down from heaven, holding in his hand the key to the bottomless pit" (20:1). The keys have changed hands, but no one will take them from the crucified and risen Messiah.

The physical description of the pit follows. With the authority of the keys that he holds, Satan opens the pit, and smoke like the smoke of a great furnace rises (9:2). However, the bottom-less pit is not "locked down," as locusts with authority like scorpions emerge and take their place "on the earth" (v. 3). The exodus is recalled in the plague of locusts (see Exod 10:3-20), but John does not develop the presence of the locusts along the lines of the Exodus account. Instead, he associates them with "the scorpions of the earth" (v. 3), well-known for the torture and pain they can inflict upon humans (see v. 5). In-deed, unlike the locusts of the Exodus plague, they are not to touch the grass, the green growth, or the trees (see Exod 10:15). A locust may destroy vegetation, but a scorpion inflicts pain on human beings. John maintains the link with the exodus in the image of the locusts, but the effects of the fall of humankind are communicated by the suffering generated by the scorpion. The first "woe" produces pain: "like the torture of a scorpion when it stings someone" (v. 5). However, those to be tortured are "only those people who do not have the seal of God on their foreheads" (v. 4). The audience recalls those sealed by God from all the tribes of Israel (7:3-8), and the multitude from the nations who have "washed their robes . . . in the blood of the Lamb" (7:9-17).

Some have "the seal of God on their foreheads." Others do not (see 7:1-8). They do not belong to "the saints" of Israel. For a period of five months, the agents that emerge from Satan's dwelling torture those who are not signed by God, but they are not to kill them. The pain is so severe that they long for death, but it is not available to them. They wish to "lose them-selves," but the agents of Satan, and even Satan himself, has no authority to grant them this blessing (v. 6). They remain locked in the pride and sinfulness that separates them from God, and they suffer because of it. John uses this imagery to describe the hopeless situation of those who reject God, a result of the fall of humankind. Satanic evil and damaging powers take control of them. This brings about incredible suffering, the result of their rejection of God, a suffering so intense that they long to be freed of it. However, the suffering endures, as they do not bear the seal of God. Only God can grant them the freedom that comes from the loss of oneself.

The rest of the "woe" is dedicated to a description of the locusts, as one image piles upon another (vv. 7-10), and to naming the location and their king (v. 11). John compares their strength to that of a battle horse (v. 7a). But however powerful, they bear a false authority, indicated by the false crowns they bear on their heads. They are not genuine crowns; they only "look like crowns," and they are falsely associated with gold that indicates the divine. The crowns look "as if" they are golden, but they are not. The demons are powerful, but they act under a false authority (v. 7). Physically their faces are human; they have hair like a woman's hair, and teeth like a lion's teeth, dressed for war, and generating a sound like that of many chariots (vv. 8-9). Despite their otherwise horrific appearance, these attributes draw them into the human sphere, and may render them more attractive to some. However, there is not a great deal that humans might find attractive in the ensemble of the description. The rest of the description imaginatively adapts the prophet Joel's description of an invading nation as locusts, "powerful and innumerable; its teeth are lion's teeth, and it has the fangs of a lioness" (Joel 1:6), with rumbling chariots arriving for battle (2:4-5). However false these appearances of authority might be, the demons come in destructive strength. They may be locusts, recalling the Exodus plague, but they behave like scorpions, with stingers in their tails "and the power to harm people for five months" (Rev 9:10), recalling v. 5.

The first "woe" closes by looking back to 9:1. The king of all the demonic creatures is "the angel of the bottomless pit": Satan. His name in Hebrew is "Abaddon," the name of a place, like Hades or Sheol, the place where Satan rules among the wicked (see Prov 15:11; Ps 88:11; Job 26:6). He has another name in Greek: "Apollyon," associated with Apollo, and bearing the meaning of "destroyer." The place where Satan rules (Hades) is associated with an experience (death). The cumulative experience of the audience teaches that the wicked angels have fallen to earth (8:6-13), that Satan possesses the keys of the great abyss from whence emerge the demons who bring unrelenting suffering to fallen humankind, from which there can be no respite (9:1-10). For the moment, Satan presides over death and Hades (9:11), but that will not always be the case (see 1:18).

# THURSDAY

*The second "woe": Destruction but the promise of salvation, God's initial intervention in Israel (9:13–11:14)*

There are three distinct moments in the second "woe." The first is the unleashing of warfare, the inevitable consequence of the fall, which brings no change of heart (9:13-21). This passage provides the biblical reading for the Thursday of the Third Week of Easter. The second is the first intervention of God in Israel, symbolized by the gift of the open scroll from the hand of an angel (10:1-11), the reading for Friday. The partial nature of this intervention is indicated in 10:7 where the angel promises that only at the blast of the seventh trumpet the mystery of God will be fulfilled. God's intervention in Israel is effective, but partial. This truth is clarified by the final moment, dedicated to the temple and the two witnesses who will be slain. But they stand again and are called "hither." Suffering and fear endure, but the God of heaven continues to be glorified (11:1-14. See vv. 7, 11-13). The *Liturgy of the Hours* uses this third moment for the Saturday of the Third Week of Easter.

*Warfare:*
*The severest consequence of the fall of humankind (9:13-21)*

As the sixth trumpet is blown, John hears a voice from the four horns of the golden altar, upon which the heavenly cult of Israel was practiced (see 8:3), commanding the trumpet-blowing angel to release "the four angels who are bound at the great river Euphrates" (vv. 13-14). The audience recalls the four angels of 7:1, holding back the four winds of the earth, so that no destruction could be done. Now they are freed from their bonds at the river Euphrates. The two are related, but in a contrasting fashion. In 7:1 they were holding back the universal destruction that could come from the four winds from the four corners of the earth. In 9:14 they are set loose, and destruction will follow. They are also fixed in a known geographical location, the Euphrates, historically regarded as the location of the beginning of organized society, the birthplace of empire. The winds of Revelation 7:1 now become angels in 9:14. As the "winds" of Daniel 7 stirred the waters to set free the four beasts that descend upon Israel, bringing war and disaster (Dan 7:4-8), the four angels are released from their bondage so that they might unleash a huge army to kill a third of humankind (Rev 9:15). The numbers of troops of cavalry, which John has heard, are incredible: two hundred million (v. 16).

A further stage has been reached: the slaying that necessarily accompanies warfare. The destruction generated by the warfare described in 9:13-21 takes place because the four angels are set free. John is addressing the issue of the war and killing that is a consequence of human sin. God is not responsible; it is the oft-repeated fruitless slaying that accompanies warfare.

The description of the horses that follows (vv. 17-19) clarifies this further. Representatives of the demonic, the horsemen are dressed for war, wearing breastplates the color of fire, sapphire, and sulfur (v. 17). Not only are they dressed for war, bearing hostile colors, but their lion-like heads breathe the smoke of the same three colors (v. 17), inflicting three plagues upon a third of humankind (v. 18). The threefold reference to the horsemen, the color of their breastplates, the smoke that issues from their mouths, and the three plagues that afflict humankind in

vv. 17 (twice) and 18 recalls the four horsemen that emerged as the first four seals were opened (6:1-8).

One color borne by the horses and their riders summoned at the opening of the seals in 6:1-8 is absent: white, the color borne by the horse and rider that emerged at the opening of the first seal (6:1-2). This was a description of human potential, wearing a crown, and coming out to conquer (6:2), only to be lost in the horses and horsemen that emerged from the following three seals (6:3-8). All such potential has been lost. At this stage of the narrative, Satan rules from the bottomless pit (9:1-12), and as a result, human beings go to war, unleashed to kill one another in massive conflicts (vv. 15-16). The fire, smoke, and sulfur that comes from the mouths of the horses causes the killing. They have power in both their mouths and their tails. Their extremities inflict harm as their tails are like serpents having heads. Their mouths exhale a killing smoke, and their serpent-like tails inflict harm (v. 19).

A further tragic consequence of the fall of humankind is described in vv. 20-21: those who are not slain in the plagues of war do not repent (v. 20). Nothing is learned from the suffering that the fall has produced. Humankind as such continues to behave in a sinful way. No one repented "of the works of their hands." Combining allusions from Daniel, Isaiah, and the Psalms, John reports that they continue to worship idols made of gold, silver, bronze, stone, and wood (see Isa 2:8, 20; 17:8; Dan 2:31-35; 4:23), but they contain no life and can give no life. They cannot "see or hear or walk" (see Ps 115:4-8). All "the inhabitants of the earth" (Rev 8:13) do not, and cannot, turn away from sin, listed as murder, sorcery, fornication, and theft. There are many forms of sin possible among humans; the ones mentioned are deeply social. The death of a third of humankind is caused by warfare (v. 15), but this suffering does not stop unrepentant human beings from inflicting death, falseness, and suffering upon one another. John has described the situation of humankind trapped in a situation of death and sin from which there is no apparent escape.

Nevertheless, even in this desperate situation, it is possible to trace slight indications of hope across this first consequence of the blowing of the sixth trumpet. Only a third of humankind is killed (v. 15). The lack of repentance (vv. 20-21) hints that better performance may still be possible. Some survive the terrors of warfare, and repentance may still be possible, despite universal hard-heartedness. The following consequences of the blowing of the sixth trumpet will expand upon that possibility (10:1-11 and 11:1-14). This must be so because God does not directly generate the death and destruction that flows from warfare. Wickedness spreads freely because Satan and his cohorts have been set free by God (vv. 14-15), and their sinful and murderous agenda has been embraced by fallen humankind (vv. 20-21). Only God's direct intervention can transform that situation.

# FRIDAY

*God's initial intervention in Israel's sacred history (10:1-11)*

The consequences of the blowing of the sixth trumpet, and the presence of the second "woe," continue into 10:1-11, and take further the narrative of the blowing of the seven trumpets. The narrative takes a more positive direction, immediately indicated by John's vision of "another mighty angel coming down from heaven" (10:1a). He descends from above, marked with heavenly trappings: wrapped in a cloud, a rainbow over his head, and a face like the sun. His power and authority are indicated by legs like pillars of fire (10:1). While the first four trumpets sent fiery angels to destroy a third of creation, the coming of the "mighty angel" from heaven bears no such threat.

The angel takes up a position that indicates a universal presence, his right foot on the sea and his left foot on the land (v. 2b), bearing a scroll in his hand (v. 2a). For the moment, John describes the scroll as "little" and "open." Recalling earlier manifestations of the divine presence, the angel utters a great shout that generates the sounding of the seven thunders (v. 3. See, for example, 4:5). This "great angel" is a positive character in the narrative, a representative of God, whose shouting unleashes the seven thunders (see Exod 19:19; 1 Sam 7:10; Jer 25:30; Hos 11:10; Joel 3:16; Amos 1:2; 3:8). What the seven thunders said, the noise of the divine presence, is not to be written down (v. 4). There is a *not yet* element in the narrative.

From his position of universal authority on sea and land, right hand raised to heaven, uttering a great confession, he swears an oath by the eternal God ("him who lives for ever and ever"), the creator of all (v. 6ab). The angel announces that the *not yet* is almost over. There will be no more delay (v. 6c). The seventh angel is about to blow his trumpet, and then "the mystery of God will be fulfilled, as he announced to his servants the prophets" (v. 7). A representative of God has proclaimed what lies at the heart of Israel's sacred history: God's initial intervention to save humankind from the disasters and destruction described by the consequences of the blowing of the trumpets. The delay is almost over (v. 6c). John is tracing God's design, the initial saving intervention of God in the gift of the Law and the witness of the prophets in Israel. It will be perfected in the fulfillment of the mystery of God (v. 7) at the blowing of the seventh trumpet: God will come, begin to reign, and destroy those who destroy the earth (see 11:17-18).

The rest of this visionary experience focuses upon the scroll in the hand of the angel (vv. 8-11). The audience recalls the earlier reference to the sealed scroll, passed from the hands of the one seated on the throne to the Lamb, the only one worthy to open the seals (5:1-14). The opening of the seals told the story of redemption of humankind, that only the Lamb was able to perform (6:1–8:1). The scroll in the hand of the mighty angel is also associated with the salvation of humankind, but it is a different scroll. In the first place it is "little." John indicates the smallness of this scroll three times (10:2, 9, 10). Compared to the scroll opened by the Lamb, it plays a lesser role. Secondly, it is already open, indicated twice (vv. 2, 8). John does not inform his audience who opened it. The fact that an angel from heaven brings with him an open scroll, of lesser significance than the scroll opened by the Lamb, indicates that the small scroll, already opened, tells of God's saving intervention in Israel, mediated by an angel. Nevertheless, the symbol of a scroll, paralleling the symbol used earlier to describe the action of Christ, the Lamb worthy to break open its seals, indicates that this is an effective intervention of God for the salvation of humankind. The fact that the scroll is open, that the angel "shouted," and the seven thunders communicate something that John wishes to write all indicate divine intervention.

John uses Ezekiel 3:1-3 creatively to clarify this further. John is to take the open scroll from the hand of the great angel, standing upon both sea and land, and eat it (vv. 9-10). The revelation is partial, as the scroll is sweet to the taste but turns bitter in the stomach (vv. 10-11). The word of God is always sweet to the taste (see Ps 19:7-10; 119:1-3; Jer 15:16), but God's initial intervention in Israel falls short of giving full satisfaction: "[M]y stomach was made bitter." The bitterness reflects a dissatisfaction with an inability fully to understand and experience the life-giving authority of the word of God. The scroll that is sweet to taste, but bitter in the stomach, indicates the graciousness of God's saving presence in Israel's sacred story, along with its limitations. The sacred history of Israel is an essential part of God's saving action, but it is incomplete. For John, it will be complete when the Law and the prophets are understood in the light of the coming of Jesus Christ. The messianic promises were made to the prophets in Israel, but they are yet to be fulfilled (v. 7). For this reason, a further prophecy must be uttered. John is told that he "must prophesy again about many peoples and nations and languages and kings" (v. 11). Ezekiel had been instructed to "speak to the house of Israel" (Ezek 3:1), excluding the other nations. The prophecy John is yet to utter, when the communication from heaven is unsealed (v. 4), is to be directed to everyone, to all the nations (see also 5:9; 7:9).

# SATURDAY

*God's presence in Israel:*
*The temple, the Law, and the prophets (11:1-14)*

John continues his creative use of the Old Testament in a positive presentation of the temple in Jerusalem. Ezekiel 40:3 (see also Zech 2:1-5) provides the general background to the measuring rod given to John, that he might "measure the temple of God and the altar and those who worship there" (Rev 11:1). Every aspect of the temple is measured in Ezekiel 40:3–42:20, but John's measurement is focused upon the "temple of God." This is an indication of the positive nature of this final moment in the consequences of the opening of the sixth trumpet, the second "woe." Unlike Ezekiel's measuring, John is asked to measure "the altar and those who worship there" (v. 1b). The focus is upon the earthly temple of Jerusalem, and the cultic activities conducted there. As in Ezekiel, the general message is clear: the Jerusalem temple reflects God's love for the nation, the place where he dwelt, their faithful and unique God. Israel's cult was effective. Mediated by an angel, the prayers of the saints of Israel rose before God (8:3-5).

However, the temple and its cult have their limitations. In the first place, John is not to measure the court outside the temple, which was "given over to the nations" (v. 2a). The cult practiced in the temple in Jerusalem came only from the Jews. It was limited to one nation; those in the outside court were excluded. Not only were they excluded, but those excluded were the pagans, the other nations, who had continually invaded Israel, destroyed the temple, and killed the people of Jerusalem. The background of Ezekiel 40–42 (and Zechariah

2:1-5) becomes especially poignant. Those prophecies were uttered *after* earlier destructions, offering the people of Israel hope with the promise that their temple would be restored in all its splendor.[1] But the return from Babylon and the restoration of Israel had been again brought to a brutal end under Antiochus IV, openly referred to by description of the trampling of the city "for forty-two months" (see Dan 7:25; 12:7).[2] Thus, John suggests, it will always be with an earthly temple. The Jerusalem temple and its cult necessarily suffered from the limitations of the vicissitudes of history, the strengths and weaknesses of cultic practices, under the direction of good or weak leadership (priests and kings), invasions, and destruction. The Jerusalem temple, so central to Israel and its cult, had come and gone at least twice (Nebuchadnezzar [597 BCE], and Antiochus IV [167 BCE]). By the time John penned Revelation, it had been devastated a third time (70 CE). It came to an end, despite the splendor of its buildings and the purity of its cult (see 8:2-5; 11:1). The unspoken premise of 11:1-2 is that such a situation will be transcended. There will be an authentic cult of the one true God not restricted to a place, measured according to its size and decoration, nor subject to the whims of human history. It will be open to the whole of humankind (see 10:11; 11:19).

Yet, with reference to Daniel's interpretation of Antiochus IV's presence, John continues the theme of violence in the narrative of the slaying and the rising of the two witnesses (vv. 3-14). As the temple, the cult, and the city were "trampled over" by foreign powers, agents of Satan who bring war and death upon humankind (v. 2. See 9:13-21), the two "witnesses" are

---

[1] Zechariah is difficult to date with precision. Most accept that there are two parts to the book. Chapters 1–9 (sometimes called First Zechariah) most likely date from 520–518 BCE, containing prophecies from the early days of the restoration of Israel after the return of the exiles from Babylon.

[2] The "forty-two months" of Revelation 11:2 appear as "a time, two times, and half a time" (12 + 24 + 6 = 42) in Daniel 7:25 and 12:7.

slain by "the beast that comes up from the bottomless pit" (11:7. See 9:1). Prior to their slaying, they have been given authority by God to prophesy for 1,260 days, dressed in the sackcloth associated with the prophetic movement (v. 3. See Mark 1:6). John identifies the two witnesses twice. In the first place, they are the "two olive trees and the two lampstands that stand before the Lord of the earth" (v. 4). These indications associate the witnesses with the temple. The lampstands have already been used as a symbol of the temple and the cult in 1:12. John freely follows and interprets Zechariah 4:3 to associate the lampstands with "the foundation of this house" (Zech 4:9). The two olive trees are also associated with the life and cult of the temple. Zechariah described them as "the two anointed ones who stand by the Lord of the whole earth" (Zech 4:14). Their initial identification is with the Jerusalem temple and its cult upon earth. They form part of God's initial saving intervention in Israel.

However, they perform an authoritative task as witnesses to the divine purpose (v. 6). The period of their ministry is 1,260 days (v. 3), equal to the "forty-two months" during which the city of Jerusalem was under attack from the foreign nations (v. 2). They are associated with the one who made fire come down from heaven (2 Kgs 1:10-12) and closed the sky to prevent rainfall (1 Kgs 17:1-7): Elijah (vv. 5-6a), and another who changed water into blood (Exod 7:14-19): Moses (v. 6b). God alleviates the death and destruction that results from the sin of humankind (9:13-21) by God's first saving intervention in Israel: the valid cultic activity of the temple, and the opened scroll taken from the hand of the great angel, consumed by John (10:1-11). The role of the two witnesses continues that theme (11:1-14). Moses and Elijah symbolize the whole of Israel's sacred history: the gift of the Law and the prophets (see v. 3). They are the "witness" (Greek: *martyria*) of God's presence in Israel, down to the coming of Jesus Christ.

John does not focus upon the historical witness of Moses and Elijah, but upon the long history of witness to the coming of Jesus that took place in the Law and the prophets. He has already indicated that a host of people from Israel exists who were "slaughtered for the word of God and the testimony they had given" (6:9). These were Israel's "saints," located under the altar, asking how much longer they must wait for God's final saving intervention (vv. 10-11). The word of God is found in the Law, and the testimony to the coming of Jesus Christ took place in the prophets of Israel (see 12:17; 14:12).

John's narrative looks back across the Old Testament witness to Jesus but is especially influenced by the suffering and death (Dan 7:1-8), and the desecration of the temple (9:26-27), associated with the time of Antiochus IV. The allusions to Danielic symbolic numbers (see Rev 11:2, 3, 9, 11: the incomplete half of a week) suggest that these recent experiences in Israel play a large role in the development of John's argument, especially as it is told in Daniel 7:7-13. As in the time of Antiochus IV, witnesses to the coming of Jesus through their loyalty to the Law, and their acceptance of the messianic prophecies, had been slain. Satan arises from his pit (see 9:1), to extend his murderous agenda (9:13-27) by making war, conquering, and slaying the witnesses (11:7). The association with Jerusalem, and the people and history of Israel, is clear in the location of the dead bodies of the slain witnesses: they lie in the street of the great city where their Lord, the one to whom they have "prophetically" born witness, was slain. But its name has been changed. The "great city" of Jerusalem is identified with two locations that tell of sin and suffering: Sodom (see Gen 18:16–20:29: sin), and Egypt (see Exod 1:8-22: suffering) (v. 8).

Even in death the sin and suffering that come from the rejection of God's promises endure. For a time that continues to allude to the persecutions of Antiochus IV, three and a half days, their bodies lie unburied. "The peoples and tribes and nations," who stamped upon the holy city and the temple (Rev 11:2), and "the inhabitants of the earth" upon whom the first two "woes" have fallen (see 8:13), rejoice in the fact that witness to the messianic promises has been silenced. The word of

God in the Law and the prophetic promises in Israel inflicted "torment" upon those who have suffered from the "woes." In their frustration they have longed for death but could not have it (see 9:6). Even in the face of death they will not repent (see 9:20-21). Nothing changes their hearts.

In this divinely directed story, judgment necessarily follows wickedness, reported in vv. 11-13. There are two responses from God: one impacts upon the witnesses (vv. 11-12), and the other upon the city of Jerusalem and its inhabitants (v. 13). There is a close association between the standing up of the slain witnesses and the death and resurrection of Jesus. In the first place, prophetically, they are slain in the same "great city," where the one to whom they bear witness was slain. John earlier described the Lamb as "standing as if it had been slaughtered" (5:6). The witnesses are called to new life, not to a return to their former life. In a fashion that parallels Ezekiel's vision of the bones that rise to life in Ezekiel 35:5, 10, "[t]he breath of life from God" enables them to "stand on their feet." For John, execution in a historical period *prior* to the historical event of the death and resurrection of Jesus does not render the saving effects of Jesus Christ's death and resurrection unavailable (see Rev 5:6; 13:8).

However, there is a difference between the death and resurrection of Jesus and the slaying and summons to life of the witnesses. God communicates life to them, just as God gave white garments to the martyrs of the fifth seal (see 6:11). The witnesses from Israel's past participate in the divine life, but they are still part of the *not yet* of the second woe. Like everyone else at this stage of John's narrative, and like the martyrs under the altar (6:9-11), they are to wait for the fulfillment of the mystery of God (10:7). The loud voice of God from heaven summons them to their place of waiting, and they ascend in a cloud "while their enemies watched them" (v. 12). God is in command, even though his mystery is not yet fulfilled. Thus, God gives a share in the divine life to the witnesses in Israel. The same message of dependence upon God is indicated by the fact that, unlike Jesus, they were not buried. Not every aspect of the unique relationship between God and the Lamb, manifested in the saving events of the death and resurrection of Jesus, is applicable to the witnesses. Those who rejected God's design, communicated in and through the Law and the prophets, are left to watch as the witnesses ascend to heaven in a cloud. The positive presentation of God's initial saving presence in the second and third sections of the second "woe" begin with an angel who *comes from* heaven "wrapped in a cloud" (10:1) and closes as the witnesses are *taken into* heaven "in a cloud" (11:12).

The enemies of the witnesses also wait, but for a very brief time: "At that moment there was a great earthquake" (11:13). An earthquake has already been associated with the death and resurrection of Jesus in the liturgy that opened the blowing of the trumpets (8:5). As we saw there, the symbol of the earthquake, associated with the death and resurrection of Jesus (see Matt 27:51-53; 28:2), is part of God's *judgment*. The slain witnesses are given life (vv. 11-12ab). Some of those who have rejected them (see v. 12c), those who dwell in the city of Jerusalem, where the witnesses were slain, are destroyed. However, not all of them; nor is the whole city destroyed. A tenth of the city falls, and the earthquake kills seven thousand people.

The destruction is partial. So also is the response of those who remain. They were terrified at what happened, and "gave glory to the God of heaven" (11:13). The partial nature of the effects of God's initial intervention in Israel continues to be narrated, limiting the devastation generated by God's judgment. God's punishment for the rejection of the witness of the Law and the prophets, as is told so often across the Hebrew Bible, leads to a brief conversion. It will not last. Despite the witnesses' death and reception of life and ascent into heaven from Jerusalem, Jesus Christ will be crucified in Jerusalem, now called Sodom and Egypt (see v. 8). For the moment, the presence of "the beast that comes up from the bottomless pit" continues to wage war against the witnesses (v. 7). Satan has not been definitively eliminated. Those who, for the moment, "gave glory to the God of heaven" will execute Jesus.

## The third "woe":
## The fulfillment of the mystery of God (11:15-19)

At the blowing of the seventh trumpet "the mystery of God will be fulfilled" (10:7). Revelation 11:15-19 provides a description of that fulfillment. In 10:7 John indicated, in a remark looking forward to the blowing of the seventh trumpet, that this mystery had been announced to his servants, the prophets. As throughout Revelation, the prophets of Israel are the bearers of the messianic promises. As the final trumpet is blown, the third "woe" reports the fulfillment of God's messianic promises in the death and resurrection of Jesus Christ: "The kingdom of the world has become the kingdom of our Lord and of his Messiah" (v. 15b). The reigning presence of the Lord and his Messiah is now located in "the kingdom of the world," during the course of human history, not at its end.[3]

A choir of loud voices in heaven proclaim that God and his Messiah have established their reign on earth (v. 15). The proclamation of the voices in heaven ceases. It is replaced by the twenty-four elders. Only they had thrones and golden crowns in the heavenly court of 4:4. As in 4:1–5:14, the elders are subordinated to their Lord (11:16). Their song proclaims the definitive establishment of God's reign (v. 17). Having taken up his great power and begun to reign, judgment necessarily follows: "The nations raged, but your wrath has come" (v. 18a). The narrative states (4:1–5:14) and restates (11:15-18) the sovereignty of the Lord and his Messiah.

---

[3] The *Liturgy of the Hours* uses 11:17-18 as the canticle for Evening Prayer: the Tuesday of all four weeks, the feasts of the Body and Blood of Christ (Evening Prayer I), the Ascension (40 days after Easter), and the Guardian Angels (2 October). It is always coupled with 12:10b-12a. See below, chapter 6, for reflections on that passage.

God's judgment has a double edge: God's servants, the prophets and the saints are rewarded (v. 18b), and those who destroy the earth are destroyed (v. 18c). The action of rewarding the prophets and the saints "and all who fear your name, both small and great" (v. 18b), refers to the period of Israel. Reward is given to those loyal to the Law (the servants), those who bore witness to the messianic promises (the prophets). A reward is granted to all who, in whatever capacity, have worked and waited faithfully for God's decisive intervention in the death and resurrection of his Son. They are the beneficiaries of the effects of the establishment of the sovereignty of God and his Messiah (v. 15).

John recalls the purveyors of evil emerging at the trumpet blasts: "those who destroy the earth" (v. 18c). Across 8:6–9:16 the powers of evil have systematically destroyed what God has created. However, God's first intervention in Israel marked a change of direction (10:1-11). The witnesses of the Law and the prophets are saved by the action of God (11:1-14), leading into the establishment of God's definitive rule (seventh trumpet: vv. 15b, 17).

The blowing of the seventh trumpet announces the "fullness" (see 10:7). For this reason, even though the seventh trumpet, as with the seventh church (see 3:20), and the seventh seal (see 8:1), proclaims God's definitive saving intervention in Jesus Christ (11:16-17), it is still a "woe." It brings destruction to those agents in the first six seals who destroy the earth and its inhabitants (v. 18c). In the gospels, Jesus' death is marked by the opening of God's temple, so that the inner sanctuary, the holy of holies, was visible to all (see Mark 15:38; Matt 27:51; Luke 23:45). For John, what results from the opening of God's temple in heaven is more specific: vision of the ark of the covenant. For the evangelists, access to God in an earthly temple is made possible for everyone by the death and resurrection of Jesus. For the early church, this event ended Israel's earthly cult.

A link with the gospels can also be sensed in the lightning and earthquake (see Mark 15:33; Matt 27:51-53; 28:2; Luke 22:44) that accompanied Jesus' death (Mark 15:33; Matt 27:51-53; Luke 22:44), and resurrection (Matt 28:2-4). However, John makes specific reference to the vision of the ark of the covenant in the heavenly temple. The death and resurrection of Jesus continues to signify the end of one cultic access to God, and the beginning of another. Nevertheless, the ark of the covenant in the heavenly temple symbolizes the never-ending relationship that God has with humankind. For John, the death and resurrection of Jesus may mark the end of one covenant and the beginning of another, but the vision of the ark of the covenant guarantees that God's relationship with humankind is everlasting.

As John closes his report of the effects of the blowing of the seventh trumpet, he looks back to the heavenly liturgy that opened this section of his book, indicating that the cultic activity of the saints on earth rose to heaven (8:2-5). As that opening heavenly liturgy closed, the narrative promised that this unique way to God was approaching its end. God's judgment was exercised as the censer filled with fire from the altar was thrown to earth (v. 5). That end has now been narrated in 11:17a. Access to God through the earthly liturgy of the temple has come to an end because the heavenly counterpart to the earthly liturgy has been transformed by the establishment of the sovereignty of God and his Messiah (vv. 15b, 17). To highlight the link between the promise of the end of Israel's cult (8:5) and its achievement (11:17a), John parallels the accompanying phenomena: "[T]here were peals of thunder, rumblings, flashes of lightning, and an earthquake" (8:5b//11:19b). The end of the cultic activity of Israel and the beginning of the Christian community form an elegant inclusion (8:2-5; 11:15-19).

# CHAPTER SIX

## *Fourth Week of Easter: Sunday through Wednesday*

### Making Sense of Revelation 12:1–14:20

The *Liturgy of the Hours* for the Sunday, Monday, Tuesday, and Wednesday of the Fourth Week of Easter is marked by three of the most dramatic passages in the book of Revelation, the woman clothed with the sun (12:1-18), the two beasts (13:1-18), and the anticipated effects of the sacrifice of the Lamb (14:1-20).[1] The literary structure of the book of Revelation depends upon the use of "sevens": letters, seals, trumpets, and bowls. Although the space given to the pouring out of the seven bowls themselves is brief (15:1–16:21) it receives the longest treatment of all the "sevens" (12:1–22:5). The three episodes of 12:1–14:20 *prepare* for the great Harmagedon (16:16) where a voice from the throne will announce, "It is done" (16:17). The three episodes that follow in 17:1–22:5 spell out the *consequences* of the pouring out of the bowls. Revelation

---

[1] The *Liturgy of the Hours* does not follow the flow of the text indicated here. The passage running from 14:1-20 is divided between Tuesday (14:1-13), and Wednesday includes the first four verses of chapter 15 (14:14–15:4). We will insert the indications of these days, but offer a continuous Easter reading of 14:1-20, followed by 15:1–16:21. For this literary structure, see above, pp. 8–11.

12:1–22:5 prepares, portrays, and spells out the consequences of the death and resurrection of Jesus Christ (15:1–16:21).

# SUNDAY

## *The woman, the son, and the dragon (12:1-6)*[2]

John describes the woman in an exalted fashion: "clothed with the sun, with the moon under her feet, and on her head a crown of twelve stars" (v. 1). But all is not well "in heaven." The woman suffers heavily from the pains of bringing forth a child: "crying out . . . in the agony of giving birth" (v. 2). John presents the woman as a symbol of beauty yet ambiguity. On the one hand she dwells splendidly in the heavenly realms. On the other, she is in pain as she attempts to bring forth a child, an image used in the Bible to describe the difficulties of spiritual birth (see Isa 26:17; 66:6-9; Jer 4:31; 13:21; John 16:21; Rom 8:22-23). The situation in Eden of God's original created human couple was not without its challenges: God forbade them access to the tree of life and the tree of knowledge (Gen 2:9, 17). A certain tension and ambiguity between humankind and God in the Genesis account can be sensed in Revelation 12:1-6. The woman's archenemy, a second portent, is also in heaven, a great red dragon with seven heads and ten horns, and a royal diadem on each head (v. 3). The red color has already been associated with the horse and its rider from the opening of the second seal: "to take peace from the earth, so that people would slaughter one another" (6:4). As grandeur and authority were part of the description of the woman, the same is the case for the dragon. The diadems worn by each of the dragon's heads matches the angelic dignity of the twenty-four elders of 4:1-11, whose heads bear

---

[2] Revelation 11:19–12:6 is used as a New Testament reading during the Liturgy of the Word for the celebration of the feast of the Assumption of Our Lady (August 15), and for votive Masses of Our Lady.

crowns. The seven heads indicate a complete set of crowned heads.

As the Lamb has seven horns (5:6), the seven heads and the ten horns of the dragon indicate that the dragon exercises great power, a power that parallels even that of the Lamb. The Lamb and the dragon will eventually lock themselves in battle. They stand for very different things. The Lamb redeems people of all tribes, nations, and languages by his blood (5:9-10). The dragon will use beastly cohorts to hold sway over humankind (see 13:1-18).

The woman in heaven may be a splendid figure, associated with the divine, but the great red dragon in heaven is equally so. His attributes associate him with other beings in the heavenly court of 4:1–5:14 and show a proximity to the Lamb. His association with the demonic is indicated by recalling the consequences of the blowing of the fourth trumpet: "His tail swept down a third of the stars of heaven and threw them to the earth" (12:4a). The hint that the blowing of the first four trumpets indicated the demonic consequences of the fall of humankind (8:12: a third of the stars lose their light) is confirmed in the description of the activity of the great red dragon.

He stands before the woman, waiting to devour her child (v. 4b). The child is born, "a son, a male child who is to shepherd all the nations with a rod of iron" (v. 5a AT). Psalm 2:9 is a royal enthronement psalm that promises the new king that he will shepherd "with a rod of iron." Psalm 2 contains YHWH's promise to a law-abiding "son" (Ps 2:7) that he will be a shepherd of his sheep, possessing the qualities of a good king. In the letter to the church at Thyatira, to "everyone who conquers" and perseveres, the promise is given: "I will give authority over the nations; to shepherd [Greek: *poimanei*] them with an iron rod, as when clay pots are shattered" (2:26-27 AT). Those who conquer and persevere will possess universal potential. The child born to the woman (12:5), whom the dragon is waiting to devour (v. 4b) is a symbol of the *potential* of humankind. The dragon plans to devour the child, to eliminate the possibility of a God-directed humankind.

The woman loses the child violently. The dragon does not destroy the potential grandeur of humankind. It is "snatched away" from the woman. The forceful nature of the Greek verb (*harpazō*) must be given its full strength. There is vigor in the action as the child is taken from the woman. There is no reason given for this detachment of the son from the woman, nor a description of sin or failure. The passive use of the verb "to snatch away" indicates the action of God. The child is subsequently located where the heavenly perfection of humankind belongs: with God and his throne (v. 5b). The threatening atmosphere of the presence of the dragon and the forceful nature of the child's being "taken away" indicate not only the frustration of the dragon, but also a loss of status on the part of the woman.

The woman, the magnificent but ambiguous bearer of the original status of humankind "in heaven," has "lost" her child. The consequence is a flight into the desert (v. 6). The woman has also "lost" her location "in heaven." She began in full splendor "in heaven" (v. 1), but now she is in flight into the desert. Her crying out in pain as she was bearing her child indicated an initial ambiguity. The ambiguity now increases as she is no longer "in heaven" but "in the desert." In the biblical tradition, the desert is an ambivalent location. The lives of major biblical personalities demonstrate its ambivalence: Abraham, Moses, the wandering Israelites, David, Elijah, and Jesus, to cite only some major examples. This tradition has its origins in Israel's experience of the exodus. The desert was a place into which the nation escaped from the slavery of Egypt, and a place of privileged encounter with God at Sinai. However, the desert was also a place of physical difficulty, temptations to return to what they had left, moral failures, the construction of false gods, disobedience, temptation, and sin.

The woman, who has lost the fruit of her womb, flees into the desert. This is a "fall" from her place in heaven, an allegory of the biblical account of the fall of humankind. With the loss of the child, the original potential for humankind to be a kingdom and priests to God (see 1:5-6) has been lost. As with the original couple, the woman finds herself in an ambivalent place, the desert. Nevertheless, this place has been prepared by God, so that she can be cared for and nourished for 1,260 days: the Danielic number for three and a half years of suffering and conflict (v. 6b. See Dan 7:25; 12:7). Sin, suffering, and conflict are part of the experience of the desert location. But God cares for her, indicated by the divine passive verb "prepared," so that God might nourish her there. Caught in an ambiguous place, God protects and nourishes her. True to the Genesis account, despite the "change of place," from heaven into an arid place resistant to the work of humankind, and threatened by the wild beasts, a place where the woman will desire her husband, bringing forth children in pain (see Gen 3:17-19), God's promises continue (see Gen 3:15-16). The destiny of humankind, symbolized by the fallen woman, is not an eternity in the desert. The period of suffering and conflict is limited: 1,260 days. Protection and promise are associated with the fall.

## *Heavenly warfare (12:7-12)*

The tradition of a heavenly battle between the good and the bad angels, so much a part of Jewish and Christian tradition, like the account of the "fall" of the woman, also has its origins in Genesis. In the primeval history, the serpent challenged the truth that no one could be like God. He affirms the opposite: to eat of the forbidden fruit would render Eve like unto God (Gen 3:5). The name of the leader of the angels in heaven who enter battle with the dragon is Michael, a Greek rendition of the Hebrew question: Who is like unto God? For the magnificent dragon and his angels, it is possible to be like unto God (Gen 3:5). The opposing angels deny that: no one is like unto God, and thus Michael and his angelic army go into battle against the dragon and his cohorts. The dragon and his angels were defeated in the heavenly battle. Because of the arrogance of the dragon and his angels, "there was no longer any place for them in heaven" (v. 8). There is no place in heaven, the dwelling place of the one and only God, for those who claim it is possible to be like unto God (Gen 3:5).

Consequently, defeated in the heavenly battle, "the great dragon was thrown down . . . thrown down to the earth, and his angels were thrown down with him" (v. 9ac). John finally unveils the identity of the dragon: "that ancient serpent, who is called the Devil and Satan, the deceiver of the whole world" (v. 9b), Satan, that ancient serpent, cast down to eat dust all the days of his life (Gen 3:14). In a highly imaginative fashion, John indicates that the casting down of the dragon from heaven to earth is the story of the fall of one of the greatest angels in the heavenly spheres: Satan, who is the devil.

Revelation 12:1-11 tells of two "falls": the fall of the woman from her exalted place in heaven, having lost the royal potential of her child, and the fall of Satan and his angels, having dared to challenge God. Shortly, John will indicate that the "earth," which received the fallen Satan and his cohorts, is the same place as "the desert" of the woman (see vv. 13-17). In the same "location" Satan pursues the woman, a snapshot of the perennially tense relationship between the powerful angelic figure, now the fallen Satan, and fragile humankind that has lost its innocence. In many ways, this is an unequal battle, but God's intervention restores the balance. As has already been indicated (v. 6), God will continue to save, protect, and nourish the woman when she flees into the desert a second time (vv. 13-16).

John hears a single "loud voice in heaven." The identity of the speaker(s) is not given but should be taken as the choir of heavenly angels, following hard on their victory of vv. 7-9. A victorious heavenly voice proclaims the establishment of "the salvation and the power and the kingdom of our God and the authority of his Messiah" (v. 10). The fall of sinful humankind and flight into an ambiguous situation, and Satan's loss of a heavenly place among his fellow angels, to take up a position as "the deceiver of the whole world" (v. 9), mark the biblical beginning of the human story, with allusion to Genesis 3–5 throughout. Once history is established, the kingdom of God, Lord, and Creator of all things must be acclaimed. Whatever about the fall of the woman and the fall of Satan, God remains Lord and Creator: "For you created all things, and by your will they existed and were created" (Rev 4:11).

The hymn also acclaims "the authority of his Messiah" (v. 10c) because the authority of the Messiah of God does not begin in the historical event of the death and resurrection of Jesus Christ, nor do the effects of his messianic role only begin with his historical death and resurrection. The voice of the conquering angels can proclaim the authority of the Messiah because the Lamb who stands with God "as if it had been slaughtered" in the heavenly court (5:6-10) was slaughtered "from the foundation of the world" (13:8). God and the Messiah belong together from the beginning of all time. The preexistence of the Messiah and the effects of his death and resurrection are challenging notions, but the falls, the flights, and the divine protection of humankind are fruit of the perennial effects of the death and resurrection of Jesus.[3]

Once the lordship of God and the authority of the Messiah have been affirmed, the loud voice from heaven can proceed to acclaim that the accuser of "our brethren," whose accusations have been brought before "our God," has been thrown down. The victory of God and his Messiah over Satan, beginning in the primeval victory of Michael and his angels (v. 11a. See 5:8-10), is an initial victory, but others will follow. In the second half of the hymn, the choir transposes the satanic presence into sacred history. Within the era of Israel's sacred history the effects of the death and resurrection of Jesus have also conquered evil and given eternal life to the holy ones of Israel. The victory described in v. 11 took place because "they have

---

[3] The *Liturgy of the Hours* regularly uses a combination of 11:17-18, 12:10b-12 as the canticle for Evening Prayer during weekly prayer and for several feasts. For detail, see above, chapter 5, note 5. For a commentary on 11:17-18, see above, chapter 5.

conquered him by the blood of the Lamb and by the word of their testimony." Many Israelites gave witness to their faith in God, especially in their loyalty to the Law, and by accepting the messianic promises of the prophets: "[T]hey did not cling to life even in the face of death" (v. 11b). Some of these witnesses gave their lives. John's message begins with an acclamation of the victory of God and his Messiah against Satan and his cohort "in heaven" (v. 10), but moves on to allude to the saints from across the history of God's chosen people (v. 11).

God's initial victory over Satan is not the end of Satan's activity. Thrown down from heaven, his threatening presence is still active as he matches his angelic authority and power against fragile humankind. Against the background of the demonic destruction of land and sea described across the blowing of the first six trumpets (8:6–11:14), the "woes" are recalled: "But woe to the earth and the sea" (12:12b). Fragile humankind is "in the desert," protected by God in trial and tribulation (v. 6). The devil has come down upon them with great wrath (v. 12b).

The devil is aware that there will be a limit to the time during which he will be free to display his devastating wrath (v. 12c). Satan, once a significant dweller in the heavenly court, knows that God will be victorious. The forces of God, under the leadership of Michael, have won the initial battle (vv. 7-9), and can rejoice. However, "on earth," "in the desert" the persecution and trials of humankind, pursued by the devil, continue.

### The woman and the dragon (12:13-17)

Both the dragon (Satan) and the woman are in the same location. Satan recognizes that he has been thrown down to the earth, and thus able to pursue the woman (v. 13). Pursued by Satan (v. 13), the woman flees into the wilderness a second time (v. 14). This is the second flight of the woman into the wilderness (see vv. 6, 14). The two flights are to be distinguished. The first flight into the wilderness was the result of the woman's fall from her place of splendor in heaven because God tore the son from her (vv. 1-2, 5). Reflecting the original "Fall," recorded in Genesis, she dwelt in the wilderness in a situation of conflict and suffering, indicated by the three and a half years, protected by God (v. 6. See Gen 2–5). Her second flight into the desert represents another stage of God's initial intervention. She finds herself in a situation of conflict and suffering, in a place where she was nourished "for a time, and times, and half a time" (v. 14).

She is carried into the wilderness on "the wings of the great eagle" and nourished there. When the great serpent issues a flood of water, to destroy her in the flood, the earth opens its mouth to swallow the river (vv. 15-16). These are unmistakable references to the exodus. The opening of the earth to swallow the flood recalls the crossing of the Red Sea (Exod 15:21-29); the nourishment in the wilderness recalls the gift of the quail and the manna (Exod 16:1-36); 19:4-8); the wings of the great eagle that carry her away from danger allude to God's presence with Israel in the desert (Exod 19:4; Deut 32:9-11). God's care for fallen humankind marked the first flight into the wilderness. The second flight is closely associated with ambiguity of Israel's experience during the exodus. There may be ambiguity in the situation of Israel, the woman (see Isa 37:22; 54:1; 62:4; Ezek 16:1ff; Hos 2:2ff; Song of Songs), a historical continuation of the primeval ambiguity of humankind once it had lost its innocence (vv. 1-2, 5-6). But the protection and care for the chosen people, the people of Israel, must be affirmed. God's promises endure, and God protects the faithful in their struggle against evil.

In the face of this situation, the dragon (the serpent, Satan) is angry with the woman: with all humankind (the first flight and protection: v. 6), and with its historical manifestation as a people of God in Israel (the second flight and protection: vv. 14-16). There is a difference, and yet an ongoing oneness, between the woman who falls from her place in heaven (humankind), and the historical experience of the woman as Israel. God's protection of Israel in the exodus does not eliminate Satan's desire to bring sin and evil into the world. The long story of God's saving intervention that began with the protection God gave to fallen humankind in Genesis (v. 6; Gen 3:16-24) continues into Israel's experience of God's presence during the exodus (vv. 14-16). Satan thus turns his attention to "the rest of her children," to bring destruction, sin, and evil into the world of "those who keep the commandments of God and hold the testimony of Jesus" (v. 17). The object of Satan's wiles will be those in Israel who hold fast to the laws of God and believe in the messianic promises of the prophets.

The dragon takes his stand "on the sand of the sea" (v. 18 AT). In his frustration, he waits, ominously, for oncoming generations. Revelation 12:1-18 *prepares* for the pouring out of the seven bowls (15:1–16:21) by providing a reflection upon the long history of the fall of humankind and Satan, coupled with God's care as Satan attacks the people of God.

# MONDAY

Straddling earth and sea (12:18), the dragon does not engage directly in the "war" against the children of the woman (12:17). Instead, he gives power to two beasts. One rises out of the sea (13:2), and the other emerges from the land (v. 11).

## *The beast from the sea (13:1-10)*

The description of the beast rising out of the sea (13:1; Dan 7:2-8) reimagines the beasts from Daniel 7. They are symbols of the political authorities who have made war against Israel, persecuted them, and subjected them to their authority: Babylon (v. 4: "like a lion and had eagles wings"), Medes (v. 5: "like a bear" [see Jer 51:11; Dan 5:30-31), Persians (v. 6: "like a leopard"), and the Seleucid dynasty (v. 7: "terrifying, and dreadful and exceedingly strong"). John combines all the symbols of the *four* kingdoms into his description of the *one* beast from the sea: "like a leopard, its feet were like a bear's, and its mouth was like a lion's mouth" (Rev 13:2a). A long history of rejection of Israel's God and persecution of God's people lies behind the indication that the seven heads carried a blasphemous name (v. 1c). Political authority "blasphemes" by making itself "like unto God."

The destructive authority of the political kingdoms of the past has been marked by a rejection of the God of Israel and attempts to impose "other gods" upon the people. The beast from the sea in Revelation 13:1-10 continues that rejection. However, the destructive authority of the beast from the sea does not originate in its own desire for power and the destruction of its enemies: "The dragon gave it his power and his throne and great authority" (v. 2b). The beast from the sea is the political agent of the dragon who conducts his diabolic affairs in history. The beast does not "represent" Satan; he is the human and earthly bearer of Satan's political agenda. He bears his blasphemous name (v. 1c). The beast from the sea is a universal representation of corrupt political authority.

God's creation is *always* threatened by *all* corrupt political authority, agents of Satan (see 8:6–9:21). The political authority challenging the book's audience at the end of the first century was the Roman Empire. The deadly wound to one of the heads that has been cured is John's way of indicating that, one after the other, the historical kingdoms, exemplified but not exhausted by those emerging from the sea in Daniel 7:1-8, rise and fall (Dan 7:11-12). Its head is mortally wounded, but restored. The demonic reality of corrupt political authority continues in many forms over the time of sacred history, and the whole earth follows these attractive powerful authorities. The capacity to remain powerfully alive and always present, despite the mortal wounds received, amazes the whole earth, and leads them to worship corrupt political authority (v. 3b). "The

Roman Empire was the confirmation and the aggravation of something which has always been present in history."[4] Corrupt political authority has *always* managed to arise from apparent death-dealing experiences: Assyria, Babylon, Medes, Persians, Alexander the Great, and the subsequent Hellenistic rulers and Romans, only to recount Israel's experiences.

The world unwittingly worships the dragon who had given his authority to the beast. Enchanted by the worldly authority of the beast from the sea (v. 3c), "the whole earth" (v. 4a) is so seduced by the seemingly invincible power of corrupt political authority that it is drawn into worship of the beast, asking the question: "Who is like the beast, and who can fight against it?" (v. 4c). No longer do the people of "the earth" recognize the ultimate authority of God "in heaven." They have been seduced into the divinization of the human and historical agent of the dragon: the beast from the sea. They cry out that nothing is more powerful than the beast; no one can fight against it (v. 4). The emissary of Satan spreads a diabolic seduction across the face of the earth through the never-ending presence of corrupt political authority. In worshipping the beast, they worship Satan/the dragon, by whose authority the beast operates in the world (v. 4a).

Like the arrogant horn that had torn out three horns to take power in Daniel 7:7 (see v. 21, with clear reference to Antiochus IV), the beast utters blasphemous and haughty words (Rev 13:5a. See Dan 7:7, 20; 11:36-39). But the passive verb, "was given" a mouth, indicates that the beast maintains his role as an eloquent agent of the dragon. The subordination of the beast shows that political authority is not *essentially* evil. All human political authority has the *potential* to be good, as everything is created by God and subordinate to God (see 4:11). It is always possible, however, that political authority can be drawn into the web of Satan and become an agent of satanic authority. For this reason, the hidden subject of these passive verbs alternates

[4] Corsini, *Apocalypse*, 234.

between Satan and God. In v. 2 the dragon "gave [the beast] his power and his throne and great authority." He continues this "gift" in the mouth that utters blasphemies. However, the limited time during which the beast will exercise his authority was also given. The context demands that this limited time is "given" from elsewhere, not from the dragon. The time frame, again from Daniel, of forty-two months (three and a half years), as elsewhere in the document (see 11:2; 11; 12:6, 14), indicates a God-determined time during which conflict and suffering take place (v. 5c. See Dan 7:25; 9:27; 12:7). In the end, no matter how devastating the worship of the beast from the sea and its consequences may prove to be, God will determine its period of ascendency.

During that God-determined time, the beast insults and blasphemes two "heavenly" realities: the existence of an all-powerful God, indicated by the use of "the name of God," and his dwelling (v. 6). The dwelling of God is not presented as the temple in Jerusalem, as the audience might expect, but as "those who dwell in heaven" (v. 6b). John describes the perennial opposition between that which is on earth, and of the earth, corrupt political authority (the beast), and that which is "in heaven," God and those who dwell in heaven. The beast from the sea behaves as if it is answerable to no other authority than the dragon who has given it authority (see v. 2, 5a, 7. See Dan 11:29-45). This is Satan's "counter-attack against the one who drove him out of his original dwelling place."[5] But this is delusion, as the way of corrupt political authority rejects the heavenly, and the lordship of God. But God will have the last word: "[I]t *was allowed* to exercise authority for forty-two months" (Rev 13:5b, emphasis added).

Having rejected God and those "in heaven," the beast turns to those "on earth" (v. 7). Following the fall of both the woman and Satan "from heaven" to earth, Satan made war on those who kept the Law of God and accepted the messianic prophecies found in Israel (12:17). This mission is now handed over

---

[5] Corsini, *Apocalypse*, 228.

to corrupt political authority. Here, the hidden subject of the verb "to hand over" is ambiguous. In God's design this is part of sacred history, a time when the faithful of Israel keep the Law and believe the promises of the prophets. But it is also the work of Satan that takes place through the beast that makes war on the saints and conquers them (v. 7).

John's original audience was not the first called to be faithful to Torah and the prophetic expectation of the coming of the Messiah. God's initial saving intervention in Israel that has produced the Christians receiving this book is crucial to John's argument. The war of corrupt political authority against "the saints" refers to a long succession of political and imperial authorities that has generated suffering and persecution for those faithful to the commandments of God, waiting for the fulfillment of the messianic promises. The book of Daniel provides a summary of the suffering of those who obeyed the commandments and listened to the prophets. The reasons for failure are stated: "We have . . . rebelled, turning aside from your commandments and ordinances. We have not listened to your servants the prophets" (Dan 9:5-6. See v. 10). John reminds his Christian readers that "the saints" of Israel, a persecuted minority, did not rebel, turn aside, or refuse to listen. They obeyed God's commandments and ordinances and listened to the prophets.

Allusion to this long period from Israel's history allows John to tell the audience of the perennial war that has gone on between corrupt political authority and "the saints." It continues to be the experience of those "on earth" keeping the commandments of God and accepting the messianic prophecies that point toward Jesus Christ (see 12:17). The beast "was given" authority over every tribe and people and language and nation, and all the inhabitants of the earth will worship it (v. 7b-8a). The origin of the beast's authority over every tribe and people and language and nation is God, who is "worthy . . . to receive glory and honor and power, for you created all things, and by your will they existed and were created" (4:11). Everything "on earth" exists because of God the creator. This also applies to the beast from the sea, political authority. As the narrative has made clear, however, Satan and his demonic agents have rebelled against their creator (12:7-9), and all the inhabitants of the earth will worship one of these agents, the beast from the sea (13:8b).

But the audience is aware that even if it has been granted by God that everyone "on earth" worships the beast (v. 8b), God has intervened into this situation definitively from the foundation of the world. Here, we must point out that the NRSV translation and the English text in the *Liturgy of the Hours* is incorrect and misleading. Most translators of the original Greek cannot accept that the Lamb was slaughtered from the foundation of the world, but that is what the original says: "And all the inhabitants of the earth will worship it, everyone whose name has not been written in the book of life of the Lamb that was slaughtered from the foundation of the world" (13:8 AT). John makes a unique contribution to early Christian thought: the saving effects of the death and resurrection of Jesus cannot be limited by time and history; they are effective "from the foundation of the world."[6]

The Lamb (5:6) has "ransomed for God saints from every tribe and language and people and nation" through the slaughtering of the Lamb (5:9). Behind the victorious activity of the beast from the sea lies the strange design of God, who grants such authority (13:7b). From the beginning of time not "everyone" has worshipped the beast, despite what is said in v. 8b. An exception is made for those whose names have been written in the book of life "of the Lamb that was slaughtered from the foundation of the world" (v. 8c AT). John looks outside the limitations of human history. For John, the life-giving salvation

[6] Readers with some knowledge of Greek will recognize this. What follows is the English of 13:8, adding the original Greek, with the claim that the slaying of the Lamb is "from the foundation of the world" underlined: "And all the inhabitants of the world will worship it, *whose name has not been written in the book of life of the Lamb that was slaughtered from the foundation of the world* (*hou ou gegraptai to onoma autou en tōi bibliōi tēs zōēs* <u>*tou arniou esphagmenou apo katabolēs kosmou*</u>).

that flows from the slaughtering of the Lamb must not be restricted to the historical period that *follows* the death of Jesus. It has been available "from the foundation of the world" (v. 8c).

The names of the "saints" who keep the commandments of God and hold fast to the messianic prophecies of the Messiah have been written in the book of life of the Lamb who was slaughtered from the foundation of the world. All whose names have not been written in that book are under the authority of the beast and worship it (v. 8). John is addressing the long history of violence and persecution, allied with the imposition of false gods by corrupt political authority. It has always marked and corrupted human history, drawing those "on earth" to accept false authority, rejecting God and all those "in heaven" (see v. 6). From all time, however, there have been some whose names have been written in the book of the Lamb slaughtered from the foundation of the world. God's initial saving intervention in Israel was always marked by the saving death and resurrection of Jesus Christ.

John directs his closing words on the beast from the sea to his readers and listeners: "Let anyone who has an ear listen" (v. 9). "If anyone is to go into captivity, into captivity you go" (v. 10a AT). What is described is the practice of the ancient principle: as you do, so will it also be done to you; the logic of violence that must be met by violence. It is the way of corrupt political authority, the way of "this world," repeated throughout human history. Reflecting the way of Jesus, the teaching of Jesus, and the teaching of the earliest church, John insists that "the saints" will not be victorious by adopting the same attitudes and practices. In the face of all the violence that corrupt political authority imposes upon "the saints," they are to meet it with endurance and faith (v. 10c).

While every tribe and people and language and nation and all the inhabitants of the earth might worship the beast (vv. 7b-8a), this is not to be the way of "the saints." They are encouraged to face the surrounding violence in the serene certitude that "the Lamb that was slaughtered before the foundation of the world" (AT) has their names inscribed in the book of life

(v. 8b). They are inscribed in the book of life as they already anticipate the event of Jesus' death. They participate in that salvific death, from all time.

> Christ's sacrifice does not come before creation according to our chronology, but in the timeless reality of God it has happened from eternity and for eternity. . . . As he knew from eternity the treachery of Satan, God had ordered from eternity the salvation of humanity by means of the sacrifice of the Lamb and the birth of a messianic figure.[7]

## The beast from the land (13:11-18)

John sees another beast, rising out of the earth. This does not mean that it follows the first beast chronologically. John saw two beasts: one from the sea (v. 1) and another from the earth (v. 11). They work as a pair. Satan has come down upon them in great wrath, through his agents (see 12:12). The ambiguity of the beast from the earth is indicated: it has two horns like a lamb, in imitation of the most significant figure in God's design for humankind, even though possessing less power; the Lamb has seven horns, while the beast that looks like a lamb has two. Despite its lamb-like appearance, the second beast spoke like a dragon. Its words are associated with the figure of Satan (v. 11). The second beast acts as a satanic figure. Despite its association with the Lamb, the beast from the earth does not exercise a saving authority, but a destructive authority that it exercises "in the presence of" the beast from the sea. The second beast exercises "all the authority" of the first beast and does so "in his presence." This beast supports and encourages the spread of the authority of the first beast, leading the earth and its inhabitants to worship that beast, the never-ending cycle of political powers (v. 12. See v. 3). There is a distance

---

[7] Edmondo F. Lupieri, *A Commentary on the Apocalypse of John*, trans. Maria Poggi Johnson and Adam Kamesar, Italian Texts and Studies on Religion and Society (Grand Rapids, MI: Eerdmans, 2009), 194.

between them, however, and it is an uncomfortable distance, indicated by the fact that the second beast is *not authorized* to act on behalf of the first beast, but does so "in his presence."

The first beast represents a long history of corrupted political authority, culminating in the audience's experience of Rome. The second beast represents a long history of corrupted religious authority that performs its rituals (vv. 13-14a), deceiving the inhabitants of the earth to make sacred images of the corrupt political powers that appear to have been destroyed, yet continue to live, culminating in the corruption of Judaism (v. 14b). Daniel continues to provide John with his background, as the erection of a statue recalls Daniel's account of Nebuchadnezzar's erection of the golden statue, demanding that all his subjects adore it (Dan 3:1-7), and Antiochus IV's placing a statue to Zeus in the Jerusalem temple (Dan 9:27). Corrupt religion's capacity to perform great signs recalls the capacity of the priests and magicians in Egypt to replicate the miraculous actions of Moses in Exodus 7:1–10:29, and the polemic between Elijah and the priests of Baal, calling down fire (see 1 Kgs 18:20-30. See also 2 Kgs 1:10).

The second beast may look like a lamb, but it speaks like a dragon. It exercises all the authority of the first beast (v. 12a) but it has not received this authority from the beast (as the first beast received the authority of the dragon in v. 2). At first sight, the mission of the second beast appears to be service to the first beast. But the second beast works for its own ends. The second beast also wants to dominate the world, but uses religious authority, in an ambiguous relationship with the first beast, to achieve that goal. It may fear the presence of the power of political authority, but it works *from its own initiative and for its own ends.*

The initiative of the beast from the land is to lead all the inhabitants of the earth to adore the first beast, to adore its image, and to receive the sign of submission to corrupt political authority by the signing of their foreheads and their hands (vv. 12-17). This is another diabolic imitation of the Lamb, who marked his followers on the forehead with the seal of the living God (7:1-8). But John points out that this second beast is given the authority "to give breath to the image of the beast who could even speak and cause those who would not worship the image of the beast to be killed" (v. 15). The beast from the land, ambiguous and corrupt religious authority, *is manipulating* corrupt political authority! The image of corrupt political authority needs corrupt religious authority to breathe and to carry out its destructive agenda. There is no symbiosis between the beast from the sea and the beast from the land; they work in a wicked collusion in which each beast seeks its own ends. But it is the religious authority that makes things happen.

The collusion established by corrupt religious authority with corrupt political authority leads to the suffering of all who do not bear the mark of the beast from the sea: "[N]o one can buy or sell who does not have the mark, that is, the name of the beast and the number of its name" (Rev 13:17). John looks back across a long history of collusion between political and religious authorities. He also focuses upon the suffering inflicted upon a Judaism that no longer could call itself God's people because it has lost its way in its selfish collusion with corrupt political authority, no longer living the commandments and listening to the prophets. John believes in an authentic Judaism, not one that hides behind the wickedness of corrupt political authority to achieve its own agenda (vv. 14-17). He has already named this form of corrupt Judaism "the synagogue of Satan" (2:9; 3:9), "Sodom and Egypt" (11:8), a corrupt religious authority that "speaks like the dragon" (13:11). Corrupt religious Judaism will eventually turn against Jesus Christ in a dramatic collusion between Roman political and Jewish religious authorities that will lead to his death.

Those who do not bear the mark of the beast from the sea, the name and the number of the beast, have suffered and have been persecuted (v. 17). In a summons that parallels v. 10c, John invites his audience to demonstrate wisdom, and "calculate the number of the beast" (v. 18a). An enigmatic indication of the human reality of the corrupt political authority closes John's reflection on the two beasts: the number 666 (v. 18). The most popular identification is the name "Nero," a name that can also equate to 666 when the letters of "Nerōn Caesar" are allocated the numbers associated with letters in the Hebrew alphabet.[8]

The NRSV translates that 666 is "the number of a person." But the Greek *arithmos gar anthrōpou estin* may indicate that this name represents a human reality, not a specific person. The number represents a simple truth. The figure "6" is one short of the number that indicates fullness: "seven." The figure "three" represents perfection. The threefold repetition of a number that falls one short of fullness indicates a human reality that forever falls frustratingly short of possible perfection.[9] Thus, 666 is a human number, representing the endlessly frustrated attempts of corrupt political authority to repeat "on earth" what its lord (the dragon) was created to be: a powerful angel "in heaven." Its rebellion and fall rendered such perfection impossible (13:4. See Gen 3:1; Rev 12:7-9, 18).

# TUESDAY

Revelation 14:1-20 provides the final *preparation* for the Harmagedon of 15:1–16:21.[10] It has two moments. The first section (vv. 1-5) is dominated by the figure of the Lamb standing on Mount Zion, surrounded by 144,000 (v. 1). The second larger section (vv. 6-20) is highlighted by the presence of Jesus Christ, who appears as "one like a Son of Man" (v. 14). Three visions

---

[8] See especially Richard Bauckham, *The Climax of Prophecy: Studies in the Book of Revelation* (Edinburgh: T. & T. Clark, 1993), 384–407.

[9] See especially G. K. Beale, *The Book of Revelation*, The New International Greek Testament Commentary (Grand Rapids, MI: Eerdmans, 1999), 721–27.

[10] The *Liturgy of the Hours* does not follow this narrative flow. See above, n. 1.

of angels take place before the centerpiece of v. 14, and three more after. The argument unfolds as follows:

*14:1-5: The Lamb who was slain before the foundation of the world (see 13:8) is surrounded by the 144,000,* the "first fruits for God and the Lamb" (v. 4).

vv. 6-20: *The prediction of the victory of the Son of Man*

    vv. 6-7: First angel: "the hour for his victory has come"

        v. 8: Second angel: announces the fall of Babylon

            vv. 9-13: Third angel: the torment of those who worship the beast, and the blessedness of those already saved in the time of Israel

*v. 14: The royal appearance of the Son of Man, armed with a sickle for the harvest*

    vv. 15-16: First angel: "the hour to reap has come"

        v. 17: Second angel: joins the harvest with a sharp sickle

            vv. 18-20: Third angel: the gathering of the vintage "outside the city," producing a blood that covers the earth

## *The Lamb and the first fruits (14:1-5)*

The Lamb appears, standing on Mount Zion, (14:1a). Reference to 5:6 is obvious, where the Lamb was presented as slain yet standing. The slain and risen Lamb, located on Mount Zion, the place of his execution but also a mountain, the biblical location of the meeting place between heaven and earth, is surrounded by the 144,000 who bear the mark of the Lamb and his Father on their foreheads (14:1b). The holy ones of Israel are praised by a voice from heaven described with the mixed, but striking, images of the sound of many waters and the sound of harpists playing on their harps. It is an authoritative divine sound: "like the sound of thunder" (v. 2). The holy ones are in the heavenly court, singing a new song generated by the uniqueness of their situation, before the four living creatures and the elders (see 4:2-11). Although the holy ones of Israel lived and died *before* the historical events of Jesus' death and resurrection, they obeyed the Law and accepted the prophets. Like the prophets before him (e.g., Hos 2; Jer 2:2:20, 28; 4:30-31; Isa 1:21; 3:15-18; Ezek 16:26-29, 23; Nah 3:4-7), John describes them as those who "have not defiled themselves with women" (v. 4a), to refer to idolatry and following false gods. It is not a vision of Christian virgins. The indication that they are followers of the Lamb "wherever he goes" (v. 4b) claims that they do more than obey the Law and listen to the prophets. Like the Lamb, they are subjected to death, witnesses in their loss of physical life. They belong to the descendants of the woman "who keep the commandments of God and hold the testimony of Jesus" (12:17). They are the "first fruits" for God and the Lamb (14:4). No lie or disobedience is found among them, and they are blameless (v. 5). They are the ones who can learn the song they sing in the heavenly court (v. 3b). One of the aims of the book of Revelation is to lead others to join that song.

## *The first group of three angels (14:6-13)*

The first three surrounding angels proclaim immutable truths. The first angel, flying in midheaven, bears the eternal Gospel of the one true God, Creator and Lord of heaven and earth. There is only one God, to whom all glory and fear is due. God is the Creator of heaven and earth, and the hour of his judgment has come (vv. 6-7). This is the "eternal Gospel" (14:6), founded upon the irreversible word of God: "I am the LORD your God who brought you out of the land of Egypt, out of the house of slavery; you shall have no other gods before me" (Exod 20:2-3). Because many have failed to accept this "eternal gospel," judgment has come (Rev 14:7).

The second angel proclaims that the judgment announced by the first angel (see v. 7) has taken place: Babylon has fallen

(v. 8). This is the first reference to a "place," a city named Babylon, whose destruction is a consequence of the pouring out of the seven bowls (see 18:1-24). The third angel describes the results of God's judgment: torment for those who worship the beast and his image (vv. 9-11), and blessings for "the saints, those who keep the commandments of God and hold fast to the faith of Jesus" (vv. 12-13).

The words of the first angel affirmed the first fundamental element of Torah (vv. 6-7; Exod 20:2-3). The words of the third angel condemn those who have committed themselves to idols and idolatrous cults: "You shall not make for yourself an idol, whether in the form of anything that is in heaven above, or that is on the earth beneath, or that is in the water under the earth. You shall not bow down to them or worship them" (Exod 20:4-5a). The loud voice of the third angel condemns all who worship the beast and its image, who bear his mark on foreheads or hands (v. 9). In the presence of the holy angels and the Lamb they will suffer the torments poured out by God's wrath, and their torment will be everlasting (vv. 10-11). The victory of the slain and risen Lamb has been in place from before the foundation of the world (5:6; 13:8), and the victory of the holy angels over Satan ended the latter's presence "in heaven" (12:7-9).

John continues to deal with this period of Israel as he points to the "endurance of the saints" (v. 12). The NRSV renders the expression as a summons, but the original Greek indicates that in the period before Christ the saints did not abandon the Law of God and the promises of the prophets (v. 12b): "Here is the endurance of the saints" (AT). This theme, already used during the opening of the fifth seal to describe those saints from Israel "under the altar" (6:9), and the offspring of the woman (12:17), is the feature of the response of Israel's holy ones to the Law and the prophets. The problem is as old as time, and many have rendered witness to the Law and the prophets by their suffering, in their death following "the Lamb wherever he goes" (v. 4).

Revelation 14:6-12 has addressed the need for the people of Israel to recognize the uniqueness of their one and only God, have no false gods, and to warn against worshipping idols. John is commanded to write that throughout Israel's sacred history, those who have died "from this time onward" have no need to wait for the historical event of the death and resurrection of Jesus. They have already died "in the Lord" (v. 13a). The Spirit of God intervenes with an affirmation that in their suffering and death, their "deeds" follow them. They will rest from their labors (v. 13b). Their names have been written in the book of life of the Lamb who was slain before the foundation of the world (13:8). In returning to this theme, John resumes the argument of 14:1-5. Already in the time of Israel, 144,000 surround the crucified and risen Lamb: "They have been redeemed from humankind as first fruits for God and the Lamb" (v. 4b). They have lived by the Law: "[T]hey are blameless" (v. 5b). The same "saints" from the story of Israel are positively described in vv. 12-13.

# WEDNESDAY

## *The One like a Son of Man (14:14)*

The appearance of "one like a Son of Man," used here for the second time (see 1:13), elevates the figure from Daniel 7:13 to divine status. He does not come with the clouds to be presented to the "Ancient One" (see Dan 7:13). He is seated upon the white cloud. He wears a golden crown on his head. He is a divine figure, who exercises judgment. The royal and divine one like a Son of Man has "a sharp sickle in his hand" (v. 14b).

For John, the death of Jesus Christ is a positive turning point in God's relationship with humankind. It brings judgment, but "reaping" with a sharp sickle, as well as indicating the destruction of the unworthy also carries with it the idea of the gathering of the chosen ones, the redemption of humankind. There is a double edge to judgment: some are "gathered"

(vv. 16-17), others are "crushed" (vv. 19-20). Rich crops and fine wine are the results of a good harvest. The sharp sickle is equivalent to the "sharp, two-edged sword" that the one like the Son of Man held in his mouth in 1:16. John has replaced the sword with a sickle in the hand of the one like the Son of Man under the influence of LXX[11] Joel 4:13: "Put in the sickle, for the harvest is ripe. Go in, tread, for the wine press is full. The vats overflow, for their wickedness is great." The crucified and risen Lamb and the one like the Son of Man effect judgment, a harvesting that will divide the good from the evil.

## *The second group of three angels (14:15-20)*

The actions of the three angels who join the one like a Son of Man in the harvesting no doubt separate the good from the bad, as the press is the wrath of God (v. 19). But a close reading of the actions of the one like a Son of Man and the second angel who wield their instruments of judgment for the "gathering of the vintage of the earth" (vv. 15-20) indicates that John's message also has a positive meaning. The harvesting done by the one like a Son of Man is a reaping of grain (vv. 15-16), and the second a reaping of grapes (vv. 17-20). Two different harvests are indicated: the harvesting of the grain (vv. 15-16) and the harvesting and pressing of the grapes (vv. 17-20).

The first angel came out of the heavenly temple, the location of the Lamb (see 4:1–5:20), and of the one like a Son of Man (see 1:16), calling out to the one like the Son of Man, the divine figure sitting on the white cloud, to reap the harvest of the earth which is now fully ripe. He does so (vv. 15-16). A ripe harvest is reaped. The reaping of the earth indicates a gathering of a summer harvest by the one like a Son of Man.

A second angel emerges from the heavenly temple. This angel plays no immediate role in the action but bears a sharp sickle (v. 17). The third angel emerges from the inner sanctum

---

[11] The Septuagint (the accepted Greek version of the Hebrew Scriptures).

of the temple, from the heavenly altar (see 5:11-12). This angel is singled out from the others as he "has authority over fire." This angel should be linked with the angel from the liturgy in heaven that opened the blowing of the seven trumpets (8:2-5). He took fire from the altar, threw it onto the earth, and judgment followed (v. 5). The theme of judgment enters the narrative.

This angel, an agent of God's judgment on the earth (see 8:2-5), commands the second angel, the bearer of the sharp sickle (see 14:17), to "gather the clusters of the vine of the earth, for its grapes are ripe" (v. 18). The second angel, the bearer of a sharp sickle, gathers the vintage from all over the earth, and throws it into "the great wine press of the wrath of God" (v. 19). The first harvesting performed by the one like a Son of Man (v. 16) does not suggest that the harvesting was punitive. Indeed, the passage may contain hints of the joyful consumption of the good fruits of the harvest of Isaiah 62:8-9 (see also 61:5-7). The vintage that results from the gathering of the clusters and the pressing of the grapes performed by the second angel (v. 19) tolls a more threatening possibility. Still echoing the image of the winepress in LXX Joel 4:13, John looks to another prophet, Isaiah 63:2-6, who told of God trampling upon his faithless people, exercising his judgment. For Isaiah, God trampled them in his wrath (v. 3), until their lifeblood poured out upon the earth (v. 6).

John persists in his allusive use of Israel's Scriptures. He manipulates these sacred texts and subordinates them to his message. The winepress is trodden "outside the city" (Rev 14:20a), alludes to the death of Jesus "outside the city" of Jerusalem (Heb 13:12; John 19:20. See Mark 15:20-22; Matt 27:31-33; Luke 23:26, 32-33; John 19:16b-17). The gathering of the vintage of the grapes by the second angel, despite the trampling and the overflow of blood (v. 20), may not be entirely negative. There is nothing negative about the gathering of the grain, as the harvest is fully ripe (vv. 15, 16). The vintage and the pressing of the grapes, however, performed by the second angel with the sharp sickle, point to judgment. The allusions to Joel and Isaiah enable John to use the winepress as a symbol of the decisive event of the judgment that flows from the crucifixion of Jesus, the Lamb (v. 1) and the one like the Son of Man (v. 14). But it is not a bloody catastrophe that will fall upon the wicked at the end of time. It is an indication that already prior to the events of Jesus Christ, the Lamb and the one like the Son of Man have gathered those who have obeyed the commandments and given witness to the coming of the Messiah and punished those who have worshipped the beast (vv. 1-20).

A positive message continues through v. 20. The blood that flows from the winepress, unlike the blood that flows from the winepress in Isaiah 63:6, is not only the result of God's wrath, but also the result of Jesus' death. The saving blood of Jesus flows for a symbolic distance of "about two hundred miles" indicating that it covers the earth (v. 20c).[12] Paradoxically, the flowing of the blood of Jesus can be positive. The death of Jesus makes available the saving effects of his death and resurrection to all people across the face of the earth. But it retains the condemnatory judgment of Isaiah 63:3-6. "The death of Christ, therefore, appears as the judgment of God in its dual aspect: the gathering of the elect (reaping) and the condemnation and destruction of the evil forces (the vintage and the pressing of the grapes)."[13]

Further allusions hide behind John's indication that the blood was "as high as a horse's bridle" (v. 20b). The audience recalls John's earlier use of the imagery of horses and horsemen. The blowing of the fifth and sixth trumpet let loose diabolical "horses": the destructive locusts "like horses equipped for battle" (9:1-11) and the innumerable death-dealing cavalry (10:13-21). The blood of the crucified Jesus flows to the height

---

[12] The Greek measurement is 1,600 stadia. Koester, *Revelation*, 626, suggests: "the imagery points to the immensity of judgment, not to geographical space."

[13] Corsini, *Apocalypse*, 272.

of the bridles of these demonic powers and stops them in their tracks. A similar allusion can be made to three of the four horses and their horsemen that appeared when the one like the Son of Man began to open the seals: the second (the red of warfare), third (the black of human deprivation), and the fourth (the pale green of death). The death of Jesus and the flow of his blood brings their progress to an end.

John has constructed 12:1–14:20 as a carefully articulated *threefold preparation* for the pouring out of the bowls.

1. The fall of the woman and Satan in 12:1-12, and the pursuit of the offspring of the woman in the ambiguity of the desert of Israel's exodus experience, at risk but protected by God (vv. 13-18), describes the perennial situation of humankind.

2. Frustrated by God's care for the woman and her offspring, throughout history Satan, unable to move freely from his fall into the great abyss, enlists the support of corrupt political (13:1-10) and corrupt religious authorities (vv. 11-18) to bring about his sinful rule. John and his readers at the end of the first century have Rome in mind, but the Satan-like presence of corrupt political and religious authority neither began nor ended with Rome.

3. Prior to the coming of Jesus Christ and his saving death and resurrection, many have lived by the Law and listened to the prophets. They have suffered and died for their witness to belief in the coming Messiah. They anticipate, participate in, and enjoy the salvific effects of the spilt blood of the Lamb, and the positive fruits that flow from the death of the Lamb and the judgment of the one like a Son of Man (14:1-5, 6-7, 12-13, 15-16, 20). But the judgment of the wicked is also assured (vv. 8-11, 17-20).

# CHAPTER SEVEN

# Fourth Week of Easter: Thursday

## Making Sense of Revelation 15:1–16:21

The climax of the "sevens," the pouring out of the bowls (15:1–16:21), is almost hidden away on the Thursday of the Fourth Week of Easter.[1] Revelation 15:1–16:21 brings the "sevens" to their dramatic conclusion. It is a powerful use of apocalyptic language and traditions to describe the death and resurrection of Jesus Christ.

# THURSDAY

### *Heavenly encounters (15:1-8)*[2]

The vision of "another portent" (see 12:1 [the woman], 3 [the dragon]), "the last" sign in heaven, it is "great and amazing" (15:1a), and it announces Jesus' victorious, yet punishing,

---

[1] The *Liturgy of the Hours* separates 15:1-4 (Wednesday) from 15:5–16:21 (Thursday). They belong together, as 15:1-8 introduces the seven angels (opening and closing with the theme of something "ended" in vv. 1 and 8), the plagues and the seven bowls are poured out in 16:1-21.

[2] The *Liturgy of the Hours* uses 15:3-4 as the canticle for Evening Prayer on the Friday of every week. It is also used for feasts: Epiphany (6 January), Pentecost, Dedication of a Church, Common of Pastors, and the Common of Men Saints.

death. The pouring out of "the wrath of God" will come to an end. John recalls the slain ones under the altar in the fifth seal (6:9-11), the 144,000 sealed from the tribes of Israel in the sixth seal (7:1-8), and the 144,000 who stand on Mount Zion with the Lamb (14:1-5), now described as "those who had conquered the beast and its image and the number of its name" (15:2b). They are described as "standing" by the sea of glass mixed by fire with harps of God in their hands. Like the Lamb (5:6; 14:1) and the two witnesses (11:11), despite violent execution, they have returned to life. As they are "in heaven," the sea of glass is the sea described during the heavenly liturgy in 4:6. It is now "mixed with fire" (v. 2a). The audience recalls the blowing of the first four trumpets during which the rebellious and fallen angels threw down fire from heaven upon the sea and the land (8:7-12). This "sea mixed with fire" is the reality that those who have conquered the beast and its image have faithfully endured, a mingling of the divine with the diabolical. They have "endured" (see 14:12) the ambiguity of Israel's history, marked by God-created human potential and the presence of the satanic.

The saints of Israel who adhered to the Law and accepted the messianic prophecies sing of the Law, the mighty deeds of justice, power, holiness, and majesty of God who must be glorified. He is King of the nations (vv. 3b, 3c, 4a), and the fulfillment of the messianic promises: God's coming messianic kingdom (v. 4bc), where God's justice and judgment will be exercised among all the nations (vv. 3c, 4c). The remaining elements of the liturgy opening, the pouring out of the bowls, take place within the heavenly temple, the model of the Jerusalem temple. The temple, further qualified as "the tent of witness" is open. The seven angels, who have the seven plagues (see Rev 15:1), come out of the open temple. Bearing the plagues, they are agents of judgment and punishment. Robed in pure linen and with golden sashes across their chests (v. 6), they are positive symbols. The angels bearing plagues, yet appearing in bright linen and wearing a golden sash,

convey a double message: punishment (the plagues) and redemption (one like a Son of Man).

A figure from the heavenly court, one of the four living
creatures (see 4:6-8), closely associated with the slain and living
Lamb (see 5:6), gives the seven angels, who already possess the
plagues, "seven golden bowls full of the wrath of God, who
lives forever and ever" (15:7). As in the days of Nebuchadnezzar, the vessels of the temple are taken, leaving the temple not
only open (v. 1), but also empty (v. 7). The plagues born by the
angels were described as being part of the final act in which
the wrath of God comes to an end in v. 1. But the heavenly
temple is filled with the divine: "smoke from the glory of God
and from his power" (v. 8), a clear reference to the consecration
of the Mosaic and the Solomonic temples (see Exod 40:32-38;
1 Kgs 8:10-11; 2 Chr 5:13-14; 7:1-3). For John, the smoke of the
glory of God fills the temple *after* it has been opened, while for
the earlier temples it marked its opening. Moses, Aaron, and
Solomon were *accompanied* with the presence of the cloud and
the smoke of the glory of the Lord. Secondly, entry and prohibition of entry into the Mosaic and Solomonic temples were
periodic, depending upon the visible presence (not able to
enter) or absence (able to enter) of the glory of God (Exod
40:34-35; 1 Kgs 8:11; 2 Chr 5:14; 7:2). Similarly, Israel could not
continue its exodus journey if the glory over the tabernacle
was absent (see Exod 40:34-38). For Revelation 15:8, the consecration of the temple is *final*; there is nothing periodic about
what is to follow. The glory of God takes over the already open
temple, and entry is impossible until after the seven angels
have poured out the wrath of God. God's relationship with
God's people is taking a new direction as the story of God's
initial saving action in Israel comes to an end, and a new era
begins.

In the seven plagues "the wrath of God is ended" (v. 1). But
God's living presence in a temple will be established "when
the seven plagues of the seven angels were ended" (v. 8c). Until
then, no one can enter the temple (v. 8b). Both punishment and
redemption will accompany the definitive end of Israel's

crucial role in the story of God's relationship with a people, its temple, and its cult. The heavenly counterpart of the earthly temple has been emptied. No further mention is made of a temple until John arrives at his description of the New Jerusalem (21:22). One period in God's salvific presence to God's people comes to an end with the end of Israel's temple, and its cult. The death and resurrection of Jesus opens a new era in the story of God's relationship with all humankind. For John, and others of his time, the earthly temple is an image of the heavenly temple. If "no one can enter" the heavenly temple, then the usefulness of the earthly temple is at an end.

## *The literary structure of 16:1-21*

The violent effects of the pouring out of the bowls depend heavily upon events that accompanied the exodus. Revelation 16:1-21 is a reflection upon the blessedness and the sinfulness that marked the story of Israel, and the reward or condemnation that flows from its being perfected and brought to closure in and through the death of Jesus Christ.

> *16:1-9: The pouring out of the first four bowls, modeled in the plagues of Egypt, directed to unrepentant worshippers of the beast from the sea.*
>
>> vv. 1-2: Sores that plague those who bore the mark of the beast and worshipped his image (see Exod 8:8-12).
>>
>> v. 3: Death-dealing blood upon everything in the sea (see Exod 7:17-24).
>>
>> vv. 4-7: The angel sings God's praises as he turns springs into blood (see Exod 7:17-24). This is "their due" because God is just.
>>
>> vv. 8-9: Scorching fire (see Exod 9:22-26), but those cursed by God do not repent (see Pharoah's hardness of heart in Exod 7:13-14, 23; 8:15, 32; 9:7, 12, 35; 10:11, 20, 27-28; 14:5-9).

16:10-21: *The pouring out of the final three bowls, culminating in*
the Lamb's saving action.

vv. 10-11: Darkness descends upon the throne of the
beast (see Exod 10:21-23), but there is no
repentance.

vv. 12-16: False signs and false prophets spread like
frogs (Exod 8:1-7). They initiate the turn of the
ages, as they gather their armies for the battle at
Harmagedon. The end is nigh: "See, I am coming
like a thief" (Rev 16:15a).

vv. 17-21: God's victory is established: earthquake, and
fury upon Babylon. Yet people curse God (v. 21).
The victory of the death of Jesus Christ is
announced: "It is done!" (v. 17).

## *The first four bowls (16:1-9)*

Out of the empty temple, the voice of God sends forth the
seven angels with the bowls to pour out his wrath (16:1). The
pouring out of the first bowl produces "a foul and painful sore"
on those who had the mark of the beast and who worshipped
its image (v. 2). The "plague" of sores that took place as the
sixth plague prior to the exodus (see Exod 8:8-12) produced
physical sores. For John they indicate a condemnation of the
"mark of the beast" upon those who bear it (see 13:16; 14:9).
Their mark of sinful adhesion has become a foul and painful
sore. Adhesion to corrupt political authority, submission to the
image of the beast erected by his agent, and corrupt religious
authority, the result of the inbreak of sin into the world (see
12:1–13:18), are condemned to failure in the eyes of God.

The pouring out of the second bowl, transforming the sea
into something like the "blood of a corpse" in which every
living thing dies, recalls the blowing of the second trumpet in
which a burning mountain was cast into the sea. A third of the
sea became blood, and a third of the living creatures died and
the ships were destroyed (see 8:8-9). But with the pouring out
of the second bowl of the wrath of God "every living thing in

the sea died" (16:3). The universality of the death, the result of the transformation of the sea into something "like the blood of a corpse," and the destruction of the dwellers in the sea point to the total destruction of the satanic powers that were cast down into the abyss (9:1-2) and the beast that rose out of the sea (13:1). A death-dealing blood is poured out upon these agents of evil; they all die (16:3).

Rivers and springs of soft water are essential for the nourishment of human beings. They have been transformed into blood by the action of God, through God's angel pouring out of the bowl of his wrath (v. 4). The angel of the waters explains what this signifies in vv. 5-6, and the altar of the temple responds in v. 7. The action of God, addressed as "O Holy One," deprives those who shed the blood of the saints and the prophets of life-giving water. Instead, he gives them blood to drink. The horrible experience of drinking blood to quench one's thirst is death-dealing. But, says the angel of the waters, this is what they deserve (v. 6). The insistence upon the righteous judgment ("true and just"), first affirmed by the angel of the waters in v. 5, is responded to by the altar, catching up the title of honor given to God in v. 5 ("O Holy One") with a further title that informs the audience of God's authority: "O Lord God, the Almighty" (v. 7). A cruel death is meted out to the beast who came from the sea, and his agent from the land (13:1-18) by the Holy One, the Lord God, the Almighty. The beast and his agent are the characters in the narrative who have "shed the blood of saints and prophets" (v. 6). God's just judgment falls upon them.

In the pouring out of the fourth bowl the power of the sun increases, scorching people with its fierce heat (vv. 8-9a). Unlike the fourth trumpet, where only a third of creation was impacted (8:12), the result of the pouring out of the fourth bowl of God's wrath is universal. The sinfulness, destruction, and ambiguity of the human situation are judged by God. Ambiguity is uncovered. However, despite the all-powerful authority of God over these plagues, many refused to repent and give glory to God (16:9b). They continue to "curse the name of God" (v. 9a).

The pouring out of all four bowls allegorizes the divine judgment upon the origin of sinfulness in the world. Here, as elsewhere, John informs his audience late in the first century that the saving judgment of God has intervened in and through the death and resurrection of Jesus, but that sinfulness, destruction, and the ambiguity of the human situation continue to exist. John insists that a new era in God's relationship with humankind began with Jesus' death and resurrection. Those who live in the period after the death and resurrection of Jesus must still recognize that many people curse the name of God, refuse to repent, and give God glory (v. 9). Revelation was written to dissuade early Christians from joining them.

## *The final three bowls (16:10-21)*

### *The fifth bowl (16:10-11)*

The pouring out of the fifth, sixth, and seventh bowls brings judgment upon the kingdom of the beast. The fifth angel pours out his bowl "on the throne of the beast," producing darkness in the whole kingdom (v. 10). An allusion to the ninth plague that preceded the exodus is present: darkness engulfed the whole of Pharaoh's kingdom (Exod 10:21-23). The throne of the beast must be the bottomless pit, into which Satan was cast in the blowing of the fifth trumpet (9:1). The pouring out of the fifth bowl, like the fourth bowl, also looks back to the smoke that rose from the shaft of the bottomless pit to darken the sun and the air, but in a reverse sense. The wrath of God poured out from the fifth bowl reduces the throne and the kingdom to complete darkness (16:10). It is God's response to the arrogance, lack of repentance, and refusal to give glory to God that marked the closure of the fourth bowl (see v. 9).

Those associated with the throne and the kingdom of the beast, now in complete darkness, gnaw their tongues in agony (v. 10c), producing pains and sores (v. 11b). Systematically, the authority of Satan is being steadily overcome as the bowls of

God's wrath are poured out. Again, however, the pouring out of the fifth bowl does not bring his adherents to conversion. They curse the God of heaven because of their suffering. They do not repent of their wicked deeds (v. 11). They maintain their adherence to the throne and the kingdom of the beast, despite its now being in complete darkness. Sinfulness that knows no turning back or repentance continues, despite the universality of the condemnatory judgment that flows from the death of Jesus Christ.

## *The sixth bowl (16:12-16)*

Both the sixth bowl and the sixth trumpet are associated with the river Euphrates (16:12; 9:14). The pouring forth of the sixth bowl dries up the river Euphrates "to prepare the way for the kings from the east" (16:12). The kings indicate the universality of kings gathering from the whole world (see v. 14). Associated with the negative result of the freeing of the angels in 9:14, the kings from the east are part of an assembly for the day of the battle "on the great day of God the almighty" (16:14). With the river that separates east from west dried up, ready to be crossed by kings from the east who will join in battle, a diabolical trinity enters the vision: the dragon, the beast, and the false prophet. This is the first time they appear together. They have been out of the action since their programmatic presentation and collusion in 12:1-18 (the dragon), 13:1-10 (the beast from the sea), and 13:11-18 (the false prophet from the land). The dragon must be present as a major player in the great battle of Harmagedon (16:16). Contrary to all expectations, this gathering of all the kings of the earth will not lead to their victory, but to a "battle on the great day of the Almighty" (v. 14c).

Alluding to the third plague that preceded the exodus (see Exod 8:1-7), three foul spirits emerge from the mouths of each of these deadly agents. They are like frogs, but they are interpreted as demonic spirits performing signs. Their demonic function is to gather the kings of the whole world in preparation for the great battle. The pouring out of all the bowls to this point has had a destructive impact upon the demonic, bringing suffering to those who follow the beast, but not repentance. As the sixth bowl is poured out a massive universal presence of wickedness assembles, kings from the east and the kings of the whole world summoned by the demonic spirits, agents of the satanic trinity of dragon, the beast from the sea, and especially the beast from the land. They continue the work of the beast from the land, spreading sinful propaganda, and going abroad to perform signs. For John, the portrait of the gathering of the demonic does not represent a single moment or event. It has been going on through the whole of human history. Satan and his agents, corrupt political authority, and corrupt religious authority have brought sin, warfare, destruction and death to humankind. John indicates that they are gathering for a final conflict, in which God will be victorious. However, many will persevere in their sinfulness despite God's decisive victory.

A parenthetic statement, articulated in the first-person singular, resonating with the words of the one like a Son of Man directed to the church in Sardis, indicates that the gathering of evil forces may have been going on since the original fall of the woman and the serpent at the beginning of the human story (12:1-9), but it is heading toward a climax. A voice addresses John's audience: "See, I am coming like a thief! Blessed is the one who stays awake and is clothed, not going about naked and exposed to shame" (v. 15). The moment of decisive judgment is upon the sinful world that has responded to the summons of the agents of the diabolical trinity of the dragon, the beast, and the false prophet (16:13): the kings from the east (v. 12), and the kings of the whole world (v. 14). As they gather, the voice rings out a warning that judgment is at hand.

But the voice also blesses all who stay awake. They are "not going about naked and exposed to shame" (v. 15c). Clothed, they walk with Jesus Christ and they are worthy (see 3:4c). The battle "on the great day of God the Almighty" is about to be engaged (v. 14c), and it will bring a judgment of destruction upon the forces of evil who have slain the saints and the prophets, and a blessing upon those who have resisted, who are clothed and are thus worthy. The warning to stay awake is a perennial message to John's audience, living in a Greco-Roman world that will neither repent, nor give honor to God (see vv. 9, 11, 21).

John's voice returns, indicating that the place for the assembly for this battle "in Hebrew is called Harmagedon" (v. 16). The reference to Megiddo is clear. This fortified city has been marked by both blessing and suffering across the history of Israel. Within the geographical world that contained Megiddo, Deborah and Barak had a victory over King Jabin of Canaan and the commander of his army, Sisera. This victory paved the way for the emergence of a nation that would become Israel (see Judg 4:1–5:31). It was also at Megiddo that the most just and God-fearing of all Israel's kings, Josiah, was slaughtered in battle with the Egyptians, under the leadership of Necho II in 609 BCE (see 2 Kgs 23:28-30). In 841 BCE King Ahaziah of Judah also died at Megiddo, fleeing there from battle, after ruling in Jerusalem for only one year (see 2 Kgs 9:27). Links with both victory and tragic losses at Megiddo may be present, especially the slaughtering of Josiah. But the critical question is the addition of the Hebrew word *har*, meaning "mountain," to the name Megiddo (Harmagedon). Megiddo was a walled city located on a plain (see Judg 5:19; 2 Chr 35:22).

As with the loss of Israel's holiest king, Josiah, at Megiddo, the death of Jesus Christ appeared to be a victory for the corrupt authorities assembled by the evil trinity of the dragon, the beast, and the false prophet. With the slaying of Josiah, evil was victorious over the good. The same could be said of the death of Jesus Christ. Associating himself with the Christian tradition that Jesus was crucified on an elevated location outside the walls of the city of Jerusalem (see John 19:20; Heb 13:12), John allegorizes another apparent victory of evil over the good. The slaying of Josiah at Megiddo is allegorized as the slaying of Jesus Christ on "Mount Megiddo (Harmagedon)" (v. 16). Enigmatically, the death of Jesus is the result of a "battle on the great day of the Lord" (v. 14) that brings about the judgment of good and evil (v. 15). The death and resurrection of Jesus are a turning point in God's dealings with humankind, an anticipated eschatological event.

## *The seventh bowl (16:17-21)*

The seventh angel poured out his bowl "into the air." The universal significance of the results of the pouring out of the seventh bowl call for a more universal recipient: the air.[3] The voice of God, a great voice from the throne of the temple (see 4:1-11), announces the victory of God: "It is done!" (v. 17. Greek: *gegonen*). Coming from different authors, and addressed to different audiences, there is a theological closeness between the final word of Jesus at the Johannine crucifixion scene (John 19:30. Greek: *tetelestai*), and the claim of the voice of God from the throne in Revelation 16:17: Jesus Christ's response to God has been completed.

There is a significant link between the pouring out of the seven bowls (16:1-21) and the blowing of the seven trumpets (8:6–11:19). During the consequences of the blowing of the sixth trumpet, the angel standing on the sea and the land, right hand raised to heaven, told John that when the seventh trumpet was blown, "the mystery of God will be fulfilled" (10:7. Greek: *etelesthē*). As with the seventh seal (see 8:1), the blowing of the seventh trumpet described the fulfillment of the mystery of God, the coming of the messianic kingdom, and the inauguration of God's universal judgment (11:15-19). But a different verb is used for "fulfillment" in 16:17 (*gegonen*). It

[3] Ian Boxall, *The Revelation of Saint John*, Black's New Testament Commentary (London: A. & C. Black, 2006), 235, helpfully suggests that "the air" has to do with "the cosmic effects of this ultimate plague."

is no longer a promise of fulfillment, but a statement of fact: it has happened.

> The Greek verb used here by John indicates something which has been fulfilled, now in a much more restricted and specific sense. It refers to the death of Christ, which forms the object of the whole of the seven of the bowls, presented here as an actual historical event.[4]

Much of what was said in the description of the fulfillment of the mystery of God in the seventh trumpet is caught up in 15:1-8 and 16:18-21. But, as happens regularly with John's practice of telling and retelling the judgment and salvation that flows from the death and resurrection of Jesus, the fulfillment of the mystery of God (10:7), the message is further developed and intensified. The seventh trumpet closed: "Then God's temple in heaven was opened, and the ark of his covenant was seen within his temple; and there were flashes of lightning, rumblings, peals of thunder, an earthquake, and heavy hail" (11:19). As we have seen, in 15:1-8, God's temple is opened, but there is no sight of the ark. Following the announcement of the completion of the salvific work of Jesus in the "It is finished!" of 16:17, John reports: "And there came flashes of lightning, rumblings, peals of thunder, and a violent earthquake" (16:17-18), and further: "huge hailstones, each weighing about a hundred pounds, dropped from heaven on people, until they cursed God for the plague of the hail, so fearful was that plague" (v. 21).

Extreme and universal violence is associated with the earthquake: "such as had not occurred since people were upon the earth" (v. 18b). Similarly, the hail is not just the "heavy hail" of 11:19, but "huge hailstones, each weighing about a hundred pounds, dropped from heaven on people" (16:21a). Recalling a series of pre-messianic prophecies uttered during the opening

---

[4] Corsini, *Apocalypse*, 305.

of the sixth seal (6:12-17), the universal impact of the pouring out of the seventh bowl leads to the elimination of all islands that flee and all mountains that disappear (v. 20). But there are further important additions to the revelation of the mystery of God from the seventh trumpet. The earthquake splits "the great city" into three parts, and the cities of the nations fell (v. 19a).

This second occurrence of the name "Babylon" (see 14:8) indicates that the city in question is Jerusalem. The city that suffered from the earthquake that took place at the death of Jesus (see Matt 27:51-53) was Jerusalem. Even more allusive yet eloquent is John's indication that "the great city" was split into three. To generate this image, John has recourse to another of his preferred prophets: Ezekiel. Ezekiel provides a sign of the destruction of Jerusalem that led to the exile in Ezekiel 5:1-4. He is instructed to shave his head and beard, and to weigh the hair (v. 1). The bundles of hair are to be divided in three: "One-third of the hair you shall burn . . . inside the city . . . one-third you shall take and strike with the sword . . . one-third you will scatter to the wind" (Ezek 5:2-3). These actions are associated with the burning of fire inside the city, the striking of the sword all around the city, and a scattering to the wind (vv. 2-3). Each third represents an action that will accompany the destruction of the city of Jerusalem that led to the exile to Babylon: "[A]nd I will unsheathe the sword after them" (v. 3b).

The judgment of God marking the fall of Jerusalem that led to the exile will be repeated with greater ferocity and universality. God's words to Ezekiel are eloquent commentary on Revelation 16:17-21: "This is Jerusalem; I have set her in the center of the nations, with countries all around her. But she has rebelled against my ordinances and my statutes. . . . [T]hus says the Lord GOD: I, I myself, am coming against you; I will execute judgments among you in the sight of the nations" (Ezek 5:5-6, 8). Earthquakes are a sign of God's judging intervention, as was seen in the opening of the sixth seal (see 6:12), and in the summoning into life of the two witnesses (see 11:13). But the earthquake described in 16:17-21 is different, and final. It is so violent that such an occurrence had never been seen before (v. 18); it destroys all the cities of the nations, the islands and the mountains, and divides Jerusalem into three (vv. 19-20).

Nevertheless, however final and decisive God's judgment that flows from the death of Jesus may be upon Jerusalem and the nations, it does not lead to repentance. The situation of the audience of Revelation is captured in John's concluding comment upon the response of those upon whom the huge hailstones fell: "[T]hey cursed God for the plague of the hail, so fearful was that plague" (v. 21b). Not even the devastating results of God's judgment upon evil enacted at the crucifixion led to conversion. John's audience, and Christian audiences of all ages, live in a situation where sinfulness continues to threaten.

Each of the "sevens" has stated and restated what the authoritative angel of the sixth trumpet has called "the mystery of God" (10:7). The announcement of the completion of God's design, and the judgment that flows from it, climaxes in 16:17-21: the pouring out of the seventh bowl. This is the fulfillment of the promise made by the one like a Son of Man in 3:20: "Listen! I am standing at the door, knocking; if you hear my voice and open the door, I will come in to you and eat with you, and you with me."

# CHAPTER EIGHT

## *Fourth Week of Easter: Friday and Saturday*

## *Fifth Week of Easter: Sunday*

### Making Sense of Revelation 17:1–19:10

As three literary units *prepared* for the pouring out of the seven bowls (Sunday to Wednesday of the Fourth Week), three further units *result from* the pouring out of the bowls (Thursday of the Fourth Week) in Revelation 17:1–22:5 (Friday and Saturday of the Fourth Week and Sunday of the Fifth Week). Elegantly constructed in three literary stages in 17:1, these consequences are opened by one of the seven angels who had the seven bowls. Another angel opens a second moment in 18:1 and a mighty angel acts against Babylon in 18:21.[1] The rider of a white horse, named "the Word of God," dominates the centerpiece of this narrative unit (19:11-16). Matching the three angels who appeared before 19:11-16, an angel opens the action in 19:17, and a further angel appears in 20:1. The narrative unit closes (in a return to 17:1) with the intervention of one of the seven angels who had the seven bowls in 21:9.[2]

---

[1] An angel appears in 17:7, but it is the same angel as 17:1, acting as an interpreter of the vision of vv. 1-6.

[2] For the purposes of this book, depending upon the use of the text from Revelation in the *Liturgy of the Hours*, chapter 8 reflects upon the first and

Not without its obscurities, attention to John's careful composition of the consequences of God's victory at Harmagedon (15:1–16:21), marked by his use of angels ([17:1; 18:1, 21] + [19:7; 20:1; 21:9]), makes the development of his argument clearer.

I. *The first consequence: The destruction of Babylon.* In 17:1: "Then one of the seven angels who had the seven bowls" opens the description of Babylon (17:1-18), and he is followed by "another angel coming down from heaven" in 18:1, announcing its destruction (18:1-20). Babylon is destroyed, as a third "mighty angel" appears in18:21, casting down a destroying "stone like a great millstone" (18:21–19:10).

*The Word of God.* Something greater than an angel enters the narrative. The section 19:11-16 is dominated by the vision of a heavenly rider on a white horse, the Word of God, judge and savior. Leading the armies of heaven, he exercises his authority in the second consequence of Jesus' death and resurrection, again marked by the presence of angels.

II. *The second consequence: The destruction of all evil power and the appearance of the New Heaven and the New Earth.* In 19:17 John turns to a vision of another angel, "standing in the sun." All corrupt earthly powers are thrown down or slain by the rider on the white horse and the armies of heaven (19:17-21). Another "angel from heaven" appears in 20:1 describing Satan's imprisonment for a long period of time, during which the holy ones of Israel share in the first resurrection. Satan reemerges in the final conflict of the death and resurrection of Jesus. His defeat leads to his being definitively cast down forever (20:1-10). The New Heaven and the New Earth, the New Jerusalem of the Christian church, emerges (21:1-8).

---

lengthiest consequence of the victory of God at Harmagedon, the destruction of Babylon (17:1–19:10). Chapter 9 will reflect upon the appearance of the rider on a white horse, and the second and third consequences (19:11–22:5).

III. *The third consequence: The gathering of the faithful in the New Jerusalem.* Returning to the opening of the first consequence (17:1), and maintaining a contact with the link between the pouring out of the bowls and the death and resurrection of Jesus, this final consequence opens in 21:9: "Then one of the seven angels who had the seven bowls" invites John to come, so that the angels might show him "the bride, the wife of the Lamb." The gift of the New Jerusalem is described across 21:9–22:5.

# FRIDAY

## *The whore seated on the beast (17:1-18)*

One of the angels who had the seven bowls announces that he will show the judgment of the great whore, seated on many waters (17:1). This is the third occasion in the narrative where "the woman" (Greek: *hē gunē*) plays an important role. In 12:1, 4, and 6, she represented the original innocence and potential of the human condition. But her son was snatched from her, as Satan waited (vv. 4-5). She fled into the wilderness, fallen from her original grandeur (v. 6). She reappears after the fall of Satan and his angels, now a symbol of Israel in the exodus, protected by God, but pursued by Satan (vv. 13, 14, 15, 16, 17). A process of more intense identification (from humankind, to Israel, to the whore) continues in 17:3, 4, 6, 7, 9, 18.

Access to the whore of 17:1 is rendered simple by her presence upon many waters that can bring those who wish to associate with her. And they have, in abundance. The kings of the earth and the inhabitants of the earth have become inebriated in their fascination with their sinful liaisons with the whore (v. 2). John is carried off "in the spirit" into a wilderness. Prophetically, he sees and speaks "in the spirit" (see Ezek 11:24). But his location "in a wilderness" places John in the location last described with the description of Satan's pursuit of the woman in 12:13-18. That woman's situation of ambiguity has now been resolved; she is no longer pursued. She has abandoned the protection of God, and has "mounted" the beast.

The description of the beast combines descriptions of both the dragon (Satan; see 12:3: red, seven heads, and ten horns) and his agent, the beast from the sea (see 13:1: seven heads and ten horns, blasphemous names). The woman is now associated with the beast from the sea, corrupt political authority, exercising the ministry of Satan. She is dressed as a prostitute, in colors that match the scarlet of the beast. In her hand she carries a golden cup, full of abominations and the impurities of her sexual license (v. 4). The description of the promiscuous activities of the woman refers to the prophetic record of Israel's sinful adherence to false gods as prostitution (see, for example, Isa 1:21; Jer 2:2, 20; 3:6, 8; 13:25; Ezek 16:15-22; 23:2-49; Hos 1:1; 2:1-13; 3:1; 5:3). The woman gives herself to the service of Satan, challenging the God of Israel with alternative gods (see 12:7-8; 13:4), and a false sense of achievement.

The woman has a name written on her forehead: "Babylon the great, mother of whores and of earth's abominations" (v. 5). She is "drunk with the blood of the saints" (v. 6). The saints and the witnesses from Israel are those who have observed the Law and gone to their death because of their acceptance of the messianic prophecies (see Dan 9:5-6, 9-10). Babylon is a symbol of Jerusalem and the corrupt political authority that dwelt there. "Babylon the great, mother of whores and of earth's abomination" (17:5) is the holy city that has abandoned God to adore false gods (the prostitute). She has slain the saints and those who waited for the fulfillment of the messianic prophecies (v. 6).

This is the reason for John's amazement (17:6c) that the angel promises to explain. The woman and the beast are a "mystery" (v. 7). The identification of the seven heads (vv. 9-11) and the ten horns (vv. 11-14) with seven mountains that are seven kings (v. 9: the seven heads) and ten lesser kings (v. 12: the ten horns) has presented difficulty for interpreters from earliest times. The description of the beast that John saw as "was and is not and is about to ascend" (v. 8a) looks back to 12:1-18 and 13:1-18, where John had vision of the majesty and power of Satan and the two beasts. All three work as one. But John also looks forward. Satan will emerge from the abyss to wreak havoc, only to be eternally contained in a lake of fire (see 20:1-10).

All the inhabitants of the earth who have committed themselves to the beast, whose names have *not been* written in the book of life from the foundation of the world, will be amazed (v. 8b). The last thing they expected was the elimination of the one who was, is not, and is yet to come. There is a close link between 17:8b and 13:8. In 13:8 the audience was told that the book of life exists because of God's gift of the Lamb who was slain before the foundation of the world. The names of "all the inhabitants of the earth" who worship the image of the beast are not found in that book. In 17:8b all the same unfortunate "inhabitants of the earth" who belong to the group identified in 13:8 will be amazed. Unlike the saints of Israel, they have not "followed the Lamb" (see 14:4), but these inhabitants of the earth are not destroyed. They may be amazed, but they do not abandon their allegiance to Satan and his agents, despite the death and resurrection of Jesus (see 16:9, 11, 21). Satan and his cohorts represent corrupt political authority and false religion and propaganda; their names are not written in the book of life. Although more universal than Rome and its empire, for John and his audience their present context was a manifestation of such political and religious corruption.

Repeating the warning that introduced the name of the beast as 666, the angel asks for a mind that has wisdom (v. 9a; see 13:18). Across vv. 9b-12 three elements (the seven heads, the beast himself, and the ten horns) taken from the description of the beast in v. 3 are identified:

- The seven heads of the satanic beast are "seven mountains on which the woman is seated" (v. 9b).

- The heads are also seven kings, "of whom five have fallen, one is living and the other is not yet come" (v. 10).

- The beast is an eighth king, belonging to the seven, and will be destroyed (v. 11).

- The ten horns are ten lesser kings who have not received a kingdom, but will have an hour of authority, in alliance with the beast (v. 12).

John's steady use of the number "seven," via allusion to Daniel 9:24-27, again comes into play. Seventy weeks are given to Israel "to finish the transgression, to put an end to sin, and to atone for iniquity, to bring in everlasting righteousness, to seal both vision and prophet and to anoint a most holy place" (v. 24). Transcending the immediate historical background that generated Daniel 9, John looks back across salvation history and sees it as a frustration of God's design for God's people and its holy city (v. 24). It has been marked by the gradual extension of the dominion of Satan (vv. 25-27). Satan's dominion has been present within history.

The seven mountains where the woman is seated indicate the culmination of the perennial powerful location of corrupt political and religious authority. Although aware of the symbolic importance of the number "seven" in Revelation, almost all interpreters incorrectly regard the association of the woman with the "seven mountains" as an allusion to Rome. In the first place, in 17:1-14 John relies heavily on the use of "seven" to indicate "completeness" (see 17:1 [twice], 7, 9 [twice], 11). The woman is intimately associated with universal and ongoing corrupt use of power. Rome certainly is part of that, and is the current problem. However, the seven mountains represent the presence of corrupt power across Israel's history, from Babylon to Rome. Interestingly, Rome has always been associated with seven "hills" (Greek: *lophos*), never with "mountains" (Greek: *oros*, as in 17:9). Werner Foerster objects to the association of *oros* with Rome: "That the hills are the hills of Rome does not fit too well." He associates himself with the importance of the use of "seven" as he suggests that they indicate "a power that spans the centuries."[3]

There is no need to identify Rome via the mention of "seven mountains." This expression is never used for Rome (founded on "seven hills"). The number "seven" has a broader reference, indicating completeness. Indeed, in the Jewish apocalypse, the First Book of Enoch, Jerusalem is described as "seven mountains" (1 Enoch 24:3-4). From a position of power on the seven mountains, across the centuries a series of kings have exercised corrupt authority, manifested in the prostitution of the woman mounted on the beast. Allusions to Imperial Rome are there, but the exercise of corrupt authority has always been present from Babylon to Rome (and beyond).

John points to the presence of corrupt political and religious authorities across the period of Israel's history that will eventually lead to battle with the Lamb (see v. 14). The beast is the ongoing presence of satanic evil represented by the dominant political authorities that marked Israel's history. It "belongs to" the seven kings because of all the evil and sinful spirits that have dominated the world, Satan and his cohorts form its consummate expression. He can be added as an eighth king who "belongs to the seven" because he embodies the wickedness they have perpetrated. The fact that Satan is the "eighth" king and will be enclosed in a lake of fire and sulfur (see 20:10, 15) suggests that his authority will reach beyond the turning point of sacred history in the death and resurrection of Jesus that brings the rule of the seven kings to an end. He may be contained, but wickedness will endure (see 16:9, 11; 22:11, 15). The ten "lesser kings" are those who have exercised their authority, however briefly, as agents of the satanic seven kings. They are not limited to agents of Rome; they indicate a series of human sovereigns who abuse their authority. They are po-

[3] Werner Foerster, "*oros*," in *Theological Dictionary of the New Testament*, ed. Gerhard Kittel and Gerhard Friedrich, trans. Geoffrey W. Bromiley, 10 vols. (Grand Rapids, MI: Eerdmans, 1964–76), 5:487.

litical figures from across the period of Israel's history who have yielded their power and authority to the beast (v. 13).

If the seven kings are the totality of evil spirits in that history, the ten lesser kings are those whose actions across human history make those evil spirits visible in the violent rejection of the Lamb (v. 14a). The satanic seven kings and their agents make war on the Lamb. But the Lamb will conquer them because he is the Lord of lords and King of kings (v. 14).

John's focus returns to the relationship between the beast and the whore in vv. 15-20. This passage, reporting the final words of the first angel, focuses upon destruction (vv. 16-17). But it is framed by statements about the universal sovereignty of the whore in v. 15 and v. 18. Seated upon the many waters (see v. 1), she is the location of "peoples and multitudes and nations and languages" (v. 15). The potential of the "great city that rules over the kings of the earth" (v. 18) is never in doubt. What she has done with that potential is another matter. "The woman" (vv. 3 and 18: *hē gunē*) is again at center stage in vv. 15-18, as she was in 17:1-2. In the literary frame generated by reference to the woman in vv. 15 and 18, however, royalty and idolatrous prostitution are linked in Jerusalem.

"The woman," presented so evocatively in 12:1 (*hē gunē*), is now described as a "whore," radically transformed from her earlier splendor because of her intimate association with the beast (17:15, see vv. 1-2). The great city that rules over the kings of the earth (v. 18, see v. 2) exercises authority because of her prostitution. "The woman" has abandoned the one true God. She has prostituted herself by her intimate association with the beast, following idols (17:1-6), rather than the Lamb. This has led the corrupt religious and political authorities of Jerusalem, in their own turn, to slay those who live by the Law, and wait upon the promises of the prophets (17:6). Among those slain by the collusion of corrupt political and religious authorities in Jerusalem is Jesus Christ (5:6; 11:8).

In a subtle and dramatic irony, the angel announces that the beast to whom the woman has committed herself by means of her own corruption and the corruption of the kings of the earth and the inhabitants of the earth will hate her, make her desolate and naked. The flesh of the woman will be devoured, and she will be destroyed by fire (v. 16). The angel announces that Jerusalem, associated with the corruption and prostitution that resulted from her mounting the beast, will be destroyed by the ten horns and the beast. This is a reference to the destruction of Jerusalem by the Roman armies in 70 CE. Hatred between the fanatical leaders of the Jewish revolt and Roman authority led to the desolation and destruction of the city and its inhabitants: "They will make her desolate and naked; they will devour her flesh and burn her up with fire" (v. 16). The city of Jerusalem went up in flames and its inhabitants suffered such incredible famine that they had recourse to cannibalism (see Josephus, *Jewish War* 6.164–168, 177–185, 228, 233–243, 250–270, 281 [fire]; *Jewish War* 5.429–38, 512, 6.193–213 [famine and cannibalism]).[4]

The action of the ten horns and the beast represents the action of the Romans, their leaders and their armies, in 70 CE (v. 16). For John, writing some twenty years after that tragedy, that historical moment was the conclusion of a long history of corruption in Jerusalem. It reached its high point in the execution of Jesus, the result of collusion between corrupt political leadership (Roman authority) and corrupt religious leadership (the Jewish leaders). Rome and its agents *represent* a specific historical moment of the perennial presence of the beast and the ten horns, corrupt political and religious authority that has dominated Jerusalem throughout the history of Israel. It led to the death of Jesus Christ.

Despite appearances to the contrary, this story came to an ironic, dramatic, and violent end because God had "put it into the hearts" of the ten horns to make possible a long history of

---

[4] Thackeray, Markus, Wikgren, Feldman, eds. *Josephus*, 3:422–25, 426–30, 440–41, 442–79, 446–55, 456–59; 3:334–37, 358–59, 432–37. Josephus reports the cannibalism of Mary, daughter of Eliazar, in *Jewish War* 201–213.

corruption. They established a kingdom of evil and handed it over to the beast that will endure "until the words of God are fulfilled" (v. 17). For John, God has allowed the perennial presence of evil among the people, the nations, the languages and the kings of this earth (17:1-2, 15, and 16), but it has come to an end. For the audience, the physical destruction of Jerusalem is a sign of the ultimate futility of humankind, with all its potential (see 12:1), entering into a corrupt association with the beast (17:1-6) to deny and execute the Messiah.

# SATURDAY

## Lament over the destruction of Jerusalem (18:1-20)

The event of the destruction of Jerusalem, with indications that recall the events of 70 CE (17:16-17: devouring flesh and burning with fire), was *seen* by John in 17:1-18. He now *hears* the tale and its consequences in 18:1–19:10. He also hears *what it means for the wicked and for the saints* (18:20; 19:1-10). These two "laments" (18:1-20; 18:21–19:10) depend upon the fact of the destruction of Jerusalem by Roman authority, already described by the angel in 17:16-17. The destruction resulted from Israel's betrayal of its God, turning to idols, and becoming part of the long tradition of wickedness and corruption, of which Rome was the current representative.

### The description of fallen Babylon (18:1-8)

The angel of 18:1 is a figure of singular significance: from heaven, having great authority, bringing brightness to the earth with his splendor. The description of the angel comes directly from Ezekiel 43:2-3, where God announced that God has come to destroy the city of Jerusalem. What has happened before happens again in the city of Jerusalem. The once beautiful and wealthy, now destroyed, is the dwelling place of foul and impure beings: demons, every foul spirit, every foul bird, and every foul and hateful beast (v. 2). The beauty that was God's design for the city has been transformed into impurity because of its fornication, the worship of false gods, shared with all the nations, the kings of the earth, and the merchants of the earth. The reason for the debasement of Jerusalem comes from the description of the behavior of the whore "with whom the kings of the earth have committed fornication, and with the wine of whose fornication the inhabitants of the earth have become drunk" (17:2). As throughout Revelation, the use of the language of prostitution indicates Israel's turning to the idols of the kings and the nations, abandoning the one true God. The same message is contained in the indication that the city is now full of demons and impurities (v. 2). Jerusalem, the dwelling place of God, has become the dwelling place of the demonic, filled with impurities.

The accusation of prostitution is not made against the merchants, but they also play their part in the distancing of the great city from its focus upon the one true God. They may have not participated in the worship of false gods, but have profited from the wealth, power, and luxury of the great city (v. 3). The fallen state of Jerusalem (v. 2) is a consequence of both the diabolic union between the woman and the beast described in 17:1-18 (18:3ab), and enabling wealth, commerce, and "this worldly" success with the merchants of this world to develop (v. 3c).

John hears "another voice from heaven" (v. 4). There are dwellers in the city that are not part of the demonic alliances of the city, and thus do not deserve to be caught up into the plagues (vv. 4, 8), the result of her sins heaped high (v. 5), and her self-glorification and indulgence in luxury. As she has indulged, so must she be punished (v. 6). These are all indications of a city that has abandoned its faith and trust in the God of Israel and has become indulgently self-focused. In calling some out of the city, the voice from heaven addresses them as "my people" (v. 4). They are to come out of the city so that they will not suffer from God's judgment upon Jerusalem's sins, but it means more than that for John's audience. To "come out" of a depraved city does not mean physical departure. Believers must continue to dwell on earth, even if they are not associated with Jerusalem's corruption, in concrete situations in the Greco-Roman world, living the in-between-time. They can "depart from the city only figuratively by actively refusing to accept its norms, values, and beliefs."[5]

God will repay her for her deeds (v. 6). Although influenced by the *lex talionis* (Exod 21:22-25; Lev 24:19-21; Deut 19:16-21), in a psalm directed against Babylon, LXX Psalm 138:8 states: "Happy shall they be who pay you back what you have done to us."[6] But the repayment will be "double" the offense. As she has lived luxuriously, God gives her a like measure of torment and grief (v. 7). From the perspective of the end of the first Christian century, John recognizes the presence of Christians living in many Greco-Roman contexts where the adoration of false gods and the luxuries that flow from commercial success determine people's relationships with God. Doubtless, Rome was one of them, but unfaithful Jerusalem serves as the model of a city whose corrupt leadership has slain Jesus and brought the city to its eventual destruction. John's audience is called to shun such behavior, and thus avoid their own destruction, wherever in the Greco-Roman world they might be living the in-between-time.

The angel cites arrogant words from the voice of the city, indicating the driving motivation for the failure of Jerusalem: "Since in her heart she says, 'I rule as a queen; I am no widow, and will never see grief' " (v. 7). The description of the destruction of Jerusalem in 70 CE (see 17:16-17) returns in 18:8b: "pestilence and mourning and famine—and she will be burned with fire." The mighty Lord who judges her cannot be denied or replaced (v. 8c). But Jerusalem has given herself over to false

---

[5] James L. Resseguie, *The Revelation of John. A Narrative Commentary* (Grand Rapids: Baker Academic, 2009), 229.

[6] See Lupieri, *Apocalypse*, 284–85. Translation of LXX Ps 138:8 from Lupieri.

gods, become entirely self-sufficient: a queen, never a widow who would see grief (v. 7b). How wrong this arrogance has proved to be! God is more powerful than any city that glories in its religious, political, and commercial self-sufficiency. This symbolic presentation of the destiny of an Israel that has succumbed to the power of corruption, out of which Christians are to exit once and for all, has taken place at the level of history in the slaying of Jesus and the destruction of Jerusalem. Babylon has fallen (v. 2). The description of the sins of the city in 18:2-8 suggests that Israel has become like all the nations and their kings. John exhorts his audience to abandon the glitter of a false trust in a Greco-Roman lifestyle, one of the results of the historical collusion between the leaders of Israel in Jerusalem, and the leaders of a long history of wickedness culminating in the current representatives of perennial corrupt political authority, Rome (v. 4). Such collusion led to the death of Jesus and the destruction of the city (17:1-18).

## Lamentations over fallen Babylon (18:9-19)

Warnings from heavenly agents disappear. They are replaced with laments from those who have profited most from the religious and economic exploitation of Jerusalem: the kings who have shared idol worship with her (fornication), introduced by the angel in v. 3 (see vv. 9-10), the merchants of the earth who have profited from her, also introduced by the angel in v. 3 (see vv. 11-14, 15-17), and the shipmasters and seafarers (vv. 18-19). (See Ezek 27:29-30, 35-36). The laments are structured in much the same way, with details altered to suit each voice.

The first to raise a lament are "the kings of the earth, who committed fornication and lived in luxury with her" (v. 9). A long history of corrupt political authorities, who have seduced Jerusalem to adopt their idols and their ways, lament that Babylon, the great city, has been so summarily destroyed. When they see the smoke of her burning, they withdraw in fear from their association with her. They wail and lament ("alas, alas!"), but stand back from her lest they be subjected to the same torment (v. 10). The merchants of the earth also weep and mourn for the city, but their motivation is purely economic. Jerusalem was once a city that purchased precious cargo from them, but they have lost their market (v. 11). The list of merchandise is impressive, made up of precious metals, stones, cloths, products of the earth, and its animal life, food, animals, and even human beings. But these luxuries, for which the soul of the city longed, manifesting its commercial corruption for its own pleasure ("your dainties and your splendor"), have been taken away forever (v. 14).

While vv. 11-14 described the response of "the merchants of the earth," representing a class of people with whom Jerusalem has traded to heighten its treasures and pleasures, vv. 15-17 addresses the lament of the merchants of each of the precious wares indicated in vv. 12-13. Their lament and their response to the destruction of Jerusalem match the response of the corrupt political and religious authorities of vv. 9-10. They also distance themselves from the city, weeping and lamenting, afraid lest they suffer the same torment (v. 15). The nature of the lament is the same (v. 15: "alas, alas!"), but their motivation is different. The rapid destruction of a once-important market has involved the destruction of their merchandise, selected from the list provided by vv. 12-13: purple and scarlet fine linen, jewels and pearls (vv. 16-17a). They may weep and lament, but there is no sign of repentance.

Political, religious, and commercial authorities lament the loss of the city they have been instrumental in corrupting (vv. 10-17). Finally, "all those whose trade is on the sea" join the lament, as they see the smoke of the burning of the destroyed city. They cry out in their sorrow that such a great city is no longer (vv. 17b-18). As with all the other laments, the rapid destruction of the city (v. 19c: "for in one hour she has been laid waste") generates sad amazement. The lament of the kings of the earth, the merchants of the earth, and the individual merchants is repeated, with the addition of gestures that demonstrate their sorrow. As well as weeping, mourning, marked by the lament (v. 19b: "alas, alas!"), they throw dust upon their heads (v. 19a. See Josh 7:6; Job 2:12; Lam 2:12). The motivation for the lament matches their loss: those whose ships had generated wealth from the city have lost access to the great city (v. 19c).

## Heaven, the saints, the sent ones, and the prophets rejoice (18:20)

The tone of lament disappears as the voice from heaven (see v. 4) commands: "[R]ejoice over her" (v. 19a). The audience knows that, however rapid and horrific, the destruction of Jerusalem is part of God's design: "For God has put it into their hearts to carry out his purpose" (17:17a). As this is the case, corrupt Jerusalem's destruction calls for rejoicing. The "heavens" are summoned to rejoice (v. 19a), and along with the heavens, the saints, those sent, and the prophets (v. 19b AT). The destruction of Jerusalem is the consequence of the liaisons, political, religious, and commercial, that have led to the desecration of Jerusalem (see v. 2; vv. 10-18). But there is more to the sad story of Jerusalem that has led to her destruction. Her wickedness has led to a long history of slaying of the saints, the sent ones of God, and the prophets (v. 19b). Joining other early Christian voices, John's voice from heaven condemns Jerusalem for its slaying of the prophets, and those sent by God (see Mark 12:1-6; Matt 22:1-6; 23:29-32; Luke 13:34). The Matthean Jesus has declared that Jerusalem is responsible for all the murders, from the beginning of time (Matt 23:35). The earthly history of Jerusalem, in collusion with corrupt powers, has generated suffering and death among God's saints, sent ones, and prophets.

John is telling his audience that the judgment upon Israel, embodied in the city of Jerusalem that has long slain the saints, those sent by God, and the prophets, has taken place (v. 20).

The leaders of the Jews in Jerusalem, in an unholy collusion with the religious, political, and commercial powers of Rome, executed Jesus. That execution was the last of a long history of unfaithful hostility. The death of Jesus brings this situation to an end (see 16:17: "It is done!"), and the destruction of Jerusalem is its consequence (see 17:16-17).

Thus, the voice from heaven can affirm that God's judgment against Jerusalem and in favor of the many who have suffered at the hands of corrupt political, religious, and commercial leadership throughout Israel's history is complete: "For God has given judgment for you against her" (v. 20c). The tense of the Greek verb "to judge" (an aorist tense) indicates that God's judging action in and through the death of Jesus has *already* justified the saints, the sent ones, and the prophets. They do not have to wait for an eschatological vindication. The destruction of Jerusalem is clear proof of that truth. The conclusion to Jerusalem's "earthly" story is destruction, the fulfillment of the will of God, and the cause of lamentation from corrupt powers (17:16-17; 18:2, 9-10, 14, 15-16, 19). But a "heavenly" world also exists. The heavens are called to rejoice, and all those who dwell in heaven, the saints, the sent ones, and the prophets who have suffered throughout Israel's sacred history, are told to join that rejoicing (v. 20).

# SUNDAY

## *Babylon is cast down (18:21-24)*

The image of a mighty angel casting down a great millstone into the sea describes the total destruction of Babylon/Jerusalem (vv. 21-22a). The totality of the destruction is indicated by the words "and will be found no more" (v. 22b), an expression that appears four times in the details that follow (see vv. 22 [twice], 23a [twice]). The consequences of the fall look back to the lamentations of vv. 9-19, but replacing a lament, the angel responsible for the casting down of Babylon utters a new reality; not only the city (v. 21), but its glories are "no more." First mentioned are the results of human activity: musical delights, the beautiful work of tradesmen, the production of fine foods from the grinding millstone, and the shining of a lantern in their midst. They are "no more" (see vv. 22-23a).

The angel then focuses upon humans themselves: the voice of the bride and the bridegroom and the successful activities of its merchants who became "the magnates of the earth." They are "no more" (v. 23bc). Part of a long history of corrupt power, successful merchants had become masters of the earth, and generated the city's glory. But the glittering success of the city was the product of deceptive sorcery (v. 23b). The use of the word "sorcery" hints that the activities of the city are associated with diabolic influence (see LXX Exod 7:11; Gal 5:20) on "all the nations." The sorrow of the laments that filled 18:9-19 has now become the sign of victory.

The "dainties" and "splendour" (v. 14) of the city have proved to be ephemeral because they have their roots in wickedness. Jerusalem has been the place where the blood of the prophets and the saints, and all on earth who have been slaughtered, has been shed (v. 24). What is spelled out in v. 24, the conclusion of this final description of the destruction of Babylon, recalls v. 20, the conclusion to the lamentations over the destruction of Babylon where the saints, sent ones, and prophets were called to rejoice because their slaughter has been vindicated by God's judgment against Jerusalem. Verses 20 and 24 look back to the long history of Jerusalem as the location *in which* the prophets and the saints have been slain (v. 24a). Jerusalem had a long history of rejecting the prophets and the saints, climaxing in the rejection and death of Jesus Christ. John identifies Jerusalem as a city led by corrupt political and religious authorities, caught up in the glitter of the Greco-Roman world that marked the city, from a time well before the violence of Antiochus IV (see 1 Macc 1:1-15), mentioned elsewhere in early Christianity (see Mark 12:1-6; Matt 22:1-6; 23:29-32).

The accusation that Babylon is responsible for the blood of all who have been slain on earth (v. 24b) warns that it is not *only* Jerusalem that has shed blood on all the earth. That city is part of a long history of corrupt cities, starting with Nineveh, and arriving at Jerusalem in its collusion with Rome. The history of Israel tells of long-standing collusions between corrupt political and religious authorities, fanned by the success of merchants and seafarers (vv. 9-19; vv. 22-23), that led to suffering and death. John now applies this to the city of Jerusalem, where the slaying of the prophets and saints eventually led to the death of Jesus, and subsequently to its own destruction in 70 CE. Across 17:1–19:10, John is telling a story well-known to his Christian audience.

## *The rejoicing of the saints of Israel (19:1-3)*[7]

John hears what seems to be "the loud voice of a great multitude in heaven" (v. 1a). The multitude of heavenly voices refers to the angelic hosts, the principal mediators between God and humankind prior to the coming of Jesus Christ. They cry out their joyful "Hallelujah" as they recognize that salvation, glory, and power come from God (v. 1b). What has just been described in the destruction of Babylon/Jerusalem is acclaimed by angels, God's agents across Israel's sacred history, aware that the judgments of God are true and just. Looking on at the destruction of Babylon/Jerusalem, they see its smoke ascend from her "forever and ever," and again cry out, "Hallelujah" (v. 3).

From the vantage point of their stage of God's saving history, the angels recognize that God has acted justly in the

---

[7] The *Liturgy of the Hours* uses a combination of the following: 19:1-2, 5-7 as the canticle for Evening Prayer on every Sunday of the year. It is also used for feasts: Easter Sunday, Pentecost Sunday, Body and Blood of Christ, Transfiguration (Evening Prayer I) (6 August), All Saints (Evening Prayer I) (1 November), Christ the King, and the Dedication of a Church during the Easter Season.

destruction of the great whore (v. 2a). On the one hand she associated with the idolatrous practices that surrounded her (v. 2b), and consequently shed the blood of the innocent servants of God who have remained true to the Law of God and who listened to the messianic prophecies (v. 2c. See 18:20, 24. See also 2 Kgs 9:7). The period of Israel, marked by the presence of its saints, sent ones, and prophets, has witnessed the corruption of Jerusalem and the slaying of these servants of God (v. 2). They now rejoice in the destruction of the city that marked the end of that period of God's intervention into human history.

### *The heavenly court rejoices (19:4-5)*

The end of one era of God's intervention and the beginning of another is captured by John's return to the imagery of the heavenly liturgy of 4:1-11. That passage described the angelic court, personified in the twenty-four elders and the four living creatures, rendering praise to God, seated on the throne as the Lord and creator of all things, through whose will everything exists (4:11). For John, the end of Israel's sacred history brings to closure the Jewish cult of that era, offered to God through the angels, who also mediated the revelation of the Law and the prophets. This "turning point of the ages" was first indicated in the opening pages of the document, when John turned away from the "loud voice" of the angel to see a face-to-face vision of the one like a Son of Man (1:10-16). It returned when John was instructed to swallow the book and commanded to prophesy once again (10:8-11). The same message of the transformation of God's mediation through word and cult returns as the twenty-four elders and the four living creatures "fell down and worshipped God who is seated on the throne" (19:4ab). Something has come to an end (4c: "Amen"), and the heavenly court rejoices as it worships (v. 4c: "Hallelujah!"). The voice of God, seated upon the throne (v. 4b), commands that all his servants, all who relate to God

with holy fear, no matter how great or small, are to praise God
(v. 5). Closely associated with the sacred history of Israel, a
new era opens with the marriage of the Lamb (see v. 7).

## The marriage of the Lamb (19:6-8)

The voice of the great multitude that John hears in v. 6 is
"like the sound of many waters." This attribute is associated
with the initial vision of the one like a Son of Man (1:15), and
the appearance of the Lamb in the company of the saints of
Israel (14:2). It is also "like a lion roaring. And when he shouted,
the seven thunders sounded," sounds that accompany the
revelation of the commands of YHWH (10:3-4). Once more
opening the utterance with a cry of joy (19:6b: "Hallelujah"),
the almighty rule of God, already at the heart of Israel's belief
(see v. 1b), calls for further joy, exultation, and glory (v. 7a).
Something beyond the unique lordship and just judgment of
God (see v. 2) is announced: "[T]he marriage of the Lamb has
come" (v. 7b).

Over against the horrific image of the union between the
beast and the woman, described as a prostitute in 17:3-5, the
voice of God announces that a union between the Lamb and
his bride (v. 7b: *hē gunē autou*) has taken place. The destruction of the woman mounted on the beast (18:9-19, 21-24) has
generated a new situation: the marriage of the Lamb and his
bride. The audience encounters a positive female figure, the
bride of the Lamb. As yet to be uncovered as the narrative
unfolds, the story of the "the bride/the woman" (*hē gunē*)
whose ambiguous situation was portrayed in 12:1-18 (*hē
gunē*), and whose wicked union with the beast further described in 17:1-3 (*hē gunē*), is taking another direction. She
has been destroyed by the beast (17:16-17), but there is still
a woman (*gunē*) in the narrative. A resolution will take place
in the identification of "the bride/the woman" with the heavenly Jerusalem in 21:9-27. The second voice of a great multitude anticipates that development in 19:7-8.

She is dressed in fine, bright, and pure linen. This adornment has been granted to her (v. 8a). It does not belong to her,
and its origins lie elsewhere. As the voice explains, "[T]he fine
linen is the righteous deeds of the saints" (v. 8b). White clothing was a sign of the salvation attained by the saints of Israel
through their observance of the Law and their acceptance of
the messianic promises of the prophets (see 6:9-11; 7:9-14). The
woman, the bride of the Lamb, receives from the Lamb a heritage of white clothing that has its origins with the "righteous
saints," both those from the history of Israel (6:11) and those
redeemed by the blood of the Lamb (7:14). There is a direct
link between the clothing of the saints of Israel and the bride
of the Lamb, the Christian community.

## *Closing dialogue (19:9-10)*

The closing dialogue between the interpreting angel and
John, the Christian writing this text, opens with a command
from the angel to the author. He is to write a beatitude (v. 9a)
that is nothing less than "true words of God" (v. 9b), a blessedness that cannot be compromised. The final establishment of
a holy people, gathered in the New Jerusalem, is announced.
God invites the faithful to the marriage supper of the Lamb.
Therein lies their blessedness. Essential to the relationship
between the Lamb and his bride, made known to the audience
in vv. 6-8, will be others who are invited to participate in the
celebration of this union. John belongs to that new situation.

Writing as a Christian at the end of the first Christian century, he takes up a position of humble receptivity before an
angel bearing a message that is nothing less than the words of
God. But the situation has changed. The angelic task of communication, essential for God's revelation in Israel, has come
to an end. John now belongs to a community of believing
Christians who give witness to what God has done in and
through the death and resurrection of Jesus. The days of the
communicating angel are over. The witness of the angel joins

the witness of Christians. One is not superior to the other; they form a single community: "I am a fellow servant with you and your comrades" (v. 10).

The interpreting angel has rendered witness to God and his Lamb throughout Israel's sacred history. Now the Christian community also bears that responsibility. They no longer need the angel as they possess the witnessing task. John and his fellow Christians are prophets. They have been given the spirit that enables authoritative witness to the divine purpose. This gift determines their mission as bearers of the witness of Jesus. The image of the angelic mediator and the prophetic mediator, bowing together in worship before the God and Father of Jesus Christ, closes the description of the destruction of Jerusalem, the first consequence of the death and resurrection of Jesus Christ (17:1–19:10). Something new is at hand.

# CHAPTER NINE

# *Fifth Week of Easter:*
# *Monday through Friday*

## Making Sense of Revelation 19:11–22:5

The readings of the Fifth Week of the Easter season proclaim God's victory and the gift of the New Jerusalem through the death and resurrection of Jesus Christ. The *Liturgy of the Hours* uses Revelation 19:11–22:5, telling of the second and third consequences of the death of Jesus. It opens with the "the Word of God," the rider of a white horse (19:11-16), followed by the interventions of three angels (19:17; 20:1, 21:9), the last of them returning to the angel who opened John's presentation of the consequences of Jesus' death 17:1: one of the seven angels who had the seven bowls (21:9).[1]

---

[1] The *Liturgy of the Hours* selects Revelation 22:1-9 as the reading for Friday of the Fifth Week of Easter. The text of Revelation indicates that 21:9–22:5 is the final moment in John's description of the consequences of the death and resurrection of Jesus. Revelation 22:6-9 serves as a "bridge," leading out of that description into the epilogue of 22:6-21. We will comment on it as part of the Saturday reading of the Fifth Week.

# MONDAY

## *Preparation for the final battle (19:11-16)*

The image of the white horse looks back to the rider on the white horse that appeared with the opening of the first seal (Rev 6:2), and the one like a Son of Man seated on the white cloud in 14:14. But the white horse of 6:2 and 19:11 are not identical. They are both associated with warfare, but the white horse of the first seal indicates humankind's potential. The rider in 19:11 is described as "Faithful and True," excelling the "potential" of humankind with his established integrity. With flaming eyes, and many diadems on his head, he is inscribed with a name known only to himself, a hint of his mysterious association with the divine, yet to be fully revealed (v. 12). John names the rider on the white horse: "the Word of God" (v. 13b). "Word of God" indicates that God communicates with humankind. John makes no claim for oneness between God and the word. He had a vision of a "word" that comes from God. The rider of the white house *functions* as a communication between God and the human situation.

In a dense chain of names and images, the Word of God is described as "clothed in a robe dipped in blood" (v. 13a), which recalls the description in 14:14 of the crowned one like a Son of Man on a white cloud bearing a sickle. In the harvest that followed from the reaping of the angels, "blood flowed from the winepress" (14:20). No doubt Isaiah 63:1-6 provides the biblical background for the presentation of the Word of God with his clothes dipped in blood. However, as we saw in the interpretation of 14:20, the blood associated with the harvest that follows the appearance of the one like a Son of Man comes from the crucifixion of Jesus Christ. It is not the blood of his destroyed enemies. The blood in which the clothing of the Word of God is dipped is the blood of Christ (19:13. See 1:5). The invincible righteous warfare and subsequent judgment that the white horse and its powerful and mysterious rider will bring about (19:11-12) are consequences of the death and resurrection of Jesus (v. 13).

The army that follows the faithful and true Word of God from the opened heaven (v. 1) is also heavenly, indicated by their garments of the white linen associated with the clothing of the bride of the Lamb in v. 8. They "follow" the rider on the white horse, mounted on their own white horses (v. 14). There is no shade of darkness in the armies of heaven that follow the one who makes known God's design (v. 13: Word of God). Imagery from earlier in the narrative returns for the further description of the nameless rider of the white horse. The one like a Son of Man, whose eyes were like flames of fire, with a two-edged sword in his mouth, spoke to each of the seven churches (see 1:12-16). The rider bears the same characteristics (19:12, 15a). Used earlier to promise the faithful in the church at Thyatira (2:27), and again to describe the potential of human-kind before the fall of the woman and Satan into the wilderness (see 12:5, 9), Psalm 2:9 appears for a third time in 19:15b. Here, however, the psalm is given a Christological interpretation to describe actions that manifest the universal authority of the heavenly rider. With an iron rod (Ps 2:9), he will strike down the nations and rule over them.

The image of the fury and wrath of God shown in the tread-ing of a winepress from 14:10, 19-20, where the salvation of the faithful in Israel was anticipated, is now applied to the role of the rider and his heavenly army (v. 15c). The name inscribed upon the horseman's robe and thigh tells the audience what has been obvious from v. 11. The rider is the "King of kings and Lord of lords" (v. 16). The unknown name of the rider may still be hidden, but his *function* in the divine economy is clear: he brings integrity (v. 11: "Faithful and True") and makes God known (v. 13b: Word of God). Along with the heavenly army that follows him (v. 14), he exercises his definitive messianic authority through the shedding of his blood (v. 13a, v. 15), thus establishing himself as King of kings and Lord of lords. His role is messianic, exercised on the cross. It will be acted out in two stages (19:17-21; 20:7-10), each of them followed by judgment (20:1-6; 20:11–21:8).

## *The first aspect of the final battle (19:17-21)*

An angel tells of the battle that follows (vv. 17-21). A mediating angel plays a crucial role. The victory of God in the first description of the battle reports from the sacred history of Israel, with specific reference to the failures of that period (19:20). Kings (see 6:15; 16:12, 14; 17:2, 10-12, 18; 18:3, 9), mighty horses and their riders (see 6:1-8), captains, the slaves and the free, the small and the great (see 6:15) have all appeared earlier in the narrative. In the battle waged in 19:17-21 the destruction of the forces of evil begins. The angel summons the birds of the air to be agents of destruction, to gorge themselves on the flesh of the wicked, free and slave, small and great (see Ezek 29:17-20). The theme of messianic destruction marks two aspects of the final battle. One follows immediately (Rev 19:19-20), fulfilling the destruction of those who have been the "destroyers of the earth" throughout Israel's history (see 11:18).

Although Harmagedon is not mentioned in the report of the first stage of the final battle (vv. 19-21), it is implied by the description of the gathering in v. 19a: "I saw the beast and the kings of the earth with their armies gathered to make war." This gathering is the result of the agents of the dragon and the beast used in John's description of the event of the death of Jesus in 16:12-14 going "abroad to the kings of the whole world, to assemble them for battle on the great day of the almighty" (v. 14). The assembly took place at Harmagedon, a symbolic reference to Golgotha, the place of Jesus' crucifixion (16:16). What is reported in 19:17-21 communicates to the audience that "the great day of the almighty" has arrived. The forces of evil engage in battle "against the rider on the [white] horse and against his army" (19:19b). The audience, aware that the rider on the white horse is True and Righteous (v. 11), the Word of God (v. 13), King of kings and Lord of lords (v. 16), whose robes are colored by his blood (v. 13), recognizes that the era of Israel has come to an end. The beast and his agent, "the false prophet," are captured (v. 20a).

Despite their apparent universal power and authority, the beast and the false prophet are cast into the lake of fire that burns with sulfur. They are now powerless but alive, despite their fiery location (v. 20c). The armies of the beast are destroyed by the sword that came from the mouth of the rider of the white horse, and their flesh is devoured to satiation by the birds of the air (v. 21). The first aspect of the final encounter between good and evil leads to the capture and the disempowering of the purveyors of evil that have been active across Israel's troubled history (vv. 20-21). Their allies are destroyed (v. 21). The beast and the false prophet remain alive but powerless (v. 20).

# TUESDAY

### *The thousand-year reign:*
### *Judgment and the "first resurrection" (20:1-6)*

John has a vision of an angel descending from heaven, bearing the key to the bottomless pit, and a great chain. Thus armed, the angel seized the dragon, for a second time named as "that ancient serpent, who is called the Devil and Satan" (see 12:9), binding him for a thousand years (20:1-2). He is cast down and locked in the bottomless pit so that his wickedness will not deceive the nations for a thousand years. Then he will be let loose for a little while (v. 3).

Crucial to an understanding of this passage, and the situation described in vv. 4-6, is a grasp of the "narrative timing" of reported episodes of the casting down of evil across Revelation. Following the flow of the narrative the audience meets, in the prologue, the description of the God-ordered final situation: the one like a Son of Man, crucified and risen, holds the keys to death and Hades (1:18). The Lamb announces to the church in Philadelphia: "These are the words of the holy one, the true one, who has the key of David, who opens and no one will shut, who shuts and no one opens" (3:7). These opening passages describe the authority of Jesus Christ in the final and definitive era of God's saving interventions, the era of the New Jerusalem.

The period *prior to this era* had suffered disorder from the initial fall of Satan, and the diabolical activity of his agents. John systematically tells and retells, with various nuances, the fall of Satan. The fall reported in 9:1-12, 14:7-13, and 18:1-24 is *always the same fall*, the result of which Satan exercises his corrupting power *through his agents* (see especially 12:1–13:18). That theme is repeated in 20:1-3. As in 12:9, where angels cast down Satan, an angel has seized, locked, and sealed "that ancient serpent, who is the Devil and Satan" (20:2). He has, for a time, been rendered powerless. This is not said of his agents, the beast, and the false prophet. The situation of the absence of Satan, bound in the abyss, will endure for a thousand years (v. 2).

The scenario of Satan fallen and rendered powerless for a thousand years (12:1-18; 20:1-3) is a prelude to the death and resurrection of the Lamb, the one like the Son of Man who has the keys of death and Hades (1:18), "who opens and no one shall shut, who shuts and no one shall open" (3:7). Once that situation is in place, subsequent to the death and resurrection of Jesus, Satan will never be "given" the keys to the bottomless pit. In short, the reign of the thousand years embraces the period of Israel, from the fall of humankind and Satan's being permitted to "be let out for a little while" (v. 3). Once cast down, losing his "reign" because of his defeat by Michael and the heavenly army (12:7-9), Satan does not exercise his diabolic influence directly. He uses his agents to spread pain, warfare, death, and wickedness across the period of Israel until he re-emerges. During this period, those who have been slain because of their observance of the Law and their acceptance of the promises of the prophets will "reign with Christ" (20:4). Only after a thousand years will Satan be unbound (v. 7)

Those who participate in the "first resurrection," described in vv. 4-6, are judged. John does not stipulate who sits upon the thrones, to whom authority to judge is given (v. 4). As the binding of Satan and the judgment delivered takes place in the period of Israel, before the historical event of the death and resurrection of Jesus, they are most likely the twenty-four elders, enthroned before the throne of God in 4:4. Those who come before the thrones for judgment are those who have been executed "for the testimony to Jesus and the word of God" (v. 4b. See 1:2, 9; 6:9; 12:17; 19:10). Israel's saints who lived by the Law ("the word of God") and accepted the messianic witness of the prophets ("testimony to Jesus") are joined by a further group of saints from the period of Israel: "They had not worshipped the beast or its image and had not received its mark on their foreheads or their hands" (v. 4c. See especially 13:12, 14-17; 14:9-11; 19:20). There are, therefore, two groups of "holy ones" whose violent death admits them to participation in the saving act of Jesus' death and resurrection: those who are executed because they live by the Law and give witness to the coming of Christ, as foretold by the prophets, and those who refuse to be deceived by the false witness, thus falling into the prostitution of idolatry. These faithful ones, even though belonging to the period of Israel's sacred history, already participate in the saving event of the death and resurrection of Jesus that has been constitutive of God's saving presence from the foundation of the world (see 5:6; 13:8).[2]

---

[2] This interpretation of the "thousand-year reign" as the period of Israel, prior to the unleashing of Satan for the final battle of Jesus' death and resurrection, challenges most interpretations of Revelation 20:1-6. The passage has troubled interpreters from the beginnings of Christianity. To this day, many Christian traditions are determined by their interpretation of the nature and the timing of "thousand-year reign" (amillenarian, premillenarian, postmillenarian, dispensationalist). For a good survey, explaining these terms and their adherents, see Koester, *Revelation*, 741–50. Like most interpreters,

Those who have been slain share in the "first resurrection": salvation through participation in Jesus' death and resurrection during the period of Israel "because of" their faithfulness to the Law, the prophets, and God (vv. 4-5). The experience of death and final "resurrection" for Israel's faithful has been dramatically presented in the account of the two witnesses (see 11:11-12). This does not indicate a resurrection from the dead, and a return to an earthly existence, but life with God, sharing in the reign of the Lamb who was slaughtered from the foundation of the world (13:8).

Not all the dead from the period of Israel share in the "first resurrection." They must wait till the thousand years have expired (v. 5a). There is no condemnation involved for "the rest of the dead" from the period of Israel. When the thousand years have expired, after the decisive victory of Jesus over Satan and his agents in and through his death and resurrection, they will share in "the second death" (v. 6. See v. 14; 21:8). For those reigning with Christ for a thousand years, Israel's slain saints, "the second death" will have no authority. They are blessed because their judgment has already taken place (see v. 4a), and they thus reign as priests of God and of Christ, in whose death and resurrection they participate, across the symbolic period of the thousand years of the era of Israel (v. 4d, v. 6c).[3]

## *The second aspect of the final battle (20:7-10)*

After explaining God's care for the "saints" of Israel, John turns to a development of the battle. Satan is released from his

---

Koester regards "the souls of those beheaded for their testimony to Jesus and for the word of God" (v. 4) as Christian martyrs, not the saints of Israel who lived by the Law and believed in the prophetic witness to Jesus Christ (as above).

[3] The "thousand years" is a symbolic number, chosen to indicate a long period of time: the era of Israel's sacred history.

prison when the thousand years, the period of Israel, comes to its end. This is part of the divine plan. Satan does not free himself. The use of the divine passive informs the audience that he is "released" by God (v. 7). The time has come to end the ambiguity that continued during the thousand years of Israel's trials. The fall of Satan and the temporary victory of Michael and his angelic army (12:7-9) is brought to its final resolution in the definitive battle between Satan, who deceives the nations from the four corners of the earth, Gog and Magog. Their huge army, numerous as the sands of the sea, gather to destroy the saints, those who have been faithful to the Law and accepted the messianic promises. They surround the saints, and the symbol of God's presence among them during the period of Israel, the beloved city of Jerusalem. This is a universal war against God and his people (see 16:14; 19:19; 20:8).

As the battle began, the beast and his agent—the false prophet—worked together (19:20). In the battle against Gog and Magog, freed by God from the abyss, in the absence of his agents, Satan works his deception alone. Gog and Magog represent people from the four corners of the earth who have succumbed to the direct deception of Satan. The war between good and evil, waged since the fall of humankind and Satan, reaches its climax as Satan and the nations he has seduced gather to destroy God's holy people and their city: "the saints and the beloved city" (v. 9a). As a result of the deceptive powers of Satan, "the nations of the four corners of the earth, Gog and Magog," wage war against God's holy ones and the holy city.

They are destroyed, consumed by fire "from heaven" (Rev 20:9). The war that has been waged across the time of Israel has led to the capture of Satan's agents and the destruction of the kings and their armies (19:20). Similarly, nations from across the face of the earth are destroyed. The final conflict between Satan, set free from the abyss, the worldly authority of the four nations, and God, ends in destruction for Satan's allies and eternal suffering for Satan. The fire from heaven continues the New Testament tradition of associating eschatological imagery with the event of the death of Jesus (see Zeph 3:8; Mark 15:33, 38; Luke 23:45, and especially Matt 27:51-54). This association with the eschatological descent of fire to destroy Satan's cohorts informs the audience that the death of Jesus is the turning point of the ages. The final victory has been won in Jesus' death and resurrection.

A result of the divine victory, the consequences for Satan—who had deceived the four corners of the earth—parallels those of the beast and the false prophet. He joins his agents, the beast, and the false prophet, who have corrupted Israel's history, in the lake of fire and sulfur (v. 10b. See 19:20). Unlike the limited time of Satan's binding in the abyss, the torment that Satan and his cohorts suffer lasts forever (v. 10c). There are two aspects of the encounter between God and evil (the beast, the false prophet, and Satan). The first looks back to the end of Israel's story at Harmagedon, the mountain of the cross of Jesus where the beast and the false prophet are defeated and cast down into the fiery lake (19:17-21). The second continues to describe the results of the encounter between evil and good. The Christian era, continuing God's sacred history, begins with God's release of Satan. In his absence, the beast and the false prophet have deceived the people and nations of their earth. God finally releases Satan to subject him to his definitive defeat in and through Jesus' cross and resurrection. Satan joins his agents, the beast from the sea and the false prophet, in the fiery lake (20:7-10).

Defeated and thrown down into the fiery lake, they suffer but they are described as "alive" (19:20; Greek: *zōntes*). When Satan joins them to suffer torment in the fiery lake these former evil powers are not annihilated. Their situation differs from the kings of the earth and their armies who joined the beast and the false prophet. Their end was clearly spelled out; they were killed by the sword and their flesh was eaten by the birds of the heavens (19:21). Destruction is also meted out to the nations from the four corners of the earth, Gog and Magog. They are destroyed, consumed by the fire from heaven that symbolized the turning point of the ages: Jesus' death and resurrection (20:9b). But this did not spell the total annihilation of Satan and his agents. They are cast down into torment, but still alive (19:20). As Adela Yarbro Collins puts it:

> The repeated rebellions of Satan impress upon the reader the irrepressible character of the forces of evil and chaos. The implication is that creation and order, peace and justice are quite fragile and partial states and that they are in constant tension with their opposites. The definitive defeat of Satan implies that even though chaos is irrepressible, it is less powerful, less real than creative order.[4]

# WEDNESDAY

## *The voice from the throne:*
## *Judgment and the "second death" (20:11–21:8)*[5]

The unconditional lordship of the judge upon the throne causes everything else, the earth and heaven, to flee from his presence. They have no place of authority or honor before the throne of God, and this flight prepares for the New Heaven and the New Earth (20:11). Returning to the literary background of Daniel 7, John summons the image of the ancient of days on the throne (Dan 7:9-10) sitting in judgment. But

---

[4] Adela Yarbro Collins, *The Apocalypse*, New Testament Message 22 (Wilmington, DE: Michael Glazier, 1979), 141.

[5] The *Liturgy of the Hours* allocates Revelation 20:1-15 to the Tuesday of the Fifth Week, and 21:1-8 to the Wednesday. John reports the second consequence of Jesus' death and resurrection in 20:15–21:8. It concludes in 20:7–21:8 where Satan's rule is definitively overcome. Several passages, indicated in what follows by a different font, are used for the Liturgy of the Word. At Masses for the dead: 20:11–21:1 and 21:1-7, Fifth Sunday of Easter in Year C: 21:1-5a, Sixth Sunday of Easter in Year C: 21:10-14, 22-23.

there are further elements in John's judgment scene: "the dead, great and small, standing before the throne" (v. 12a).

As in Daniel 7:9-10, the books are opened, but a further element is added to the Danielic scene, taken from the narrative of Revelation itself. Not only are the books of judgment opened (see Dan 7:10), but another book—the book of life—is opened. The theme of a "book" has appeared consistently throughout Revelation (3:4; 5:9; 13:8; 17:8). A set of books are the heavenly records of all human deeds. These books list all the dead, great and small, who stand before the throne of judgment (20:12a). The names of the redeemed are recorded in the book of life. The opening of this book enables right judgment (v. 12b). One book records the deeds of all humankind. Another, the book of life, contains the names of those who are saved.

The universality of this judgment of the dead is described. The sea, the abyss from which the beast emerges, gives up its dead. Death and Hades (see 1:18) also give up their dead. These are "symbolic expressions to indicate the wicked powers which live in those places and which move to torment, subjugate and slay the men who live on earth (see 6:8; 9:1ff; 13:1ff)."[6] Judgment is universal as even these authoritative powers, now overcome, give up their dead (v.13a). God is judging the performance of *all the dead* (v. 13a). Given the narrative to this point, the threat of salvation or condemnation depends upon one's adhesion to Satan and his agents, or faithfulness to the Law and acceptance of the messianic promises of the prophets.

Death and Hades are cast into the lake of fire (v. 14). Repeating the same message, but focusing upon the people and not the place, John reports that anyone among the dead whose name was not written in the book of life (see 17:8; 20:12) is also thrown into the lake of fire (20:15). This moment

---

[6] Corsini, *Apocalypse*, 383.

of judgment of the dead that assigns them to the lake of fire is "the second death" (v. 14). Physical death is an obvious first "ending" to human life and experience. But God's judgment upon the attachments of the dead while they were alive (v. 13: "all were judged according to what they had done") is final: a "second death."

Only those whose names are not found in the book of life are condemned to the lake of fire. There are others whose names are found in the book of life (see 3:5; 13:8; 17:8), saved by the death and resurrection of Jesus Christ. They have passed through physical death, but they must undergo the process of judgment that is the "second death." Some from the period of Israel already participate in this salvation through their death for Torah and the witness of the prophets. They are not exposed to the "second death" (see 20:6). But others from this era are also waiting: "The rest of the dead did not come to life until the thousand years were ended" (20:5). All except that unique group of martyrs from Israel's past history must face the judgment of the "second death" (vv. 14-15). They will be judged by what they have done (v. 13).

As throughout the episodes that tell of God's definitive victory over evil, angels play no role in the description of the positive aspect of the judgment that flows from God's decisive victory over evil (see 20:7, 11). God has intervened directly in the death and resurrection of Jesus. John sees something entirely new: a New Heaven and a New Earth. The heaven and earth that have circumscribed the world, its nations, and its peoples, under the sway of the powers of evil, have passed away (see 19:20-21; 20:10, 14-15). The sea, from which the beast emerged, is no more (21:1). The death and resurrection of Jesus have created a new world.

The "newness" of this creative act of God does not negate the grandeur of God's original creation, as described in Genesis 1:1–2:4a. That grandeur was spoiled by the arrogance of Satan and the beginning of a history of sin (Gen 2:4b–3:24). The new creation of heaven and earth in Revelation 21:1 is a "renewal" of God's original creative design. As the voice from the throne explains: "See, I am making all things new" (v. 5). The holy city of the New Jerusalem descends into this renewed creation. The city comes out of heaven and is thus from God. No intermediaries are called for. One of the abiding hopes of Israel, and the promise of the prophets, was the restoration of the holy city and its temple. John continues that prophetic tradition but renders the city and its temple a spiritual reality. Although experienced on earth, it transcends a given time and place.

On the last occasion in the narrative where the Jerusalem temple appeared, it had been emptied of its adornment and its cultic activity. It waited for the seven bowls to be poured out (15:1-8). That series of events, symbolically telling of the death and resurrection of Jesus, has now taken place (see 16:17: "It is done!"). As he introduces the theme of the New Jerusalem, John does not report the physical destruction of the old Jerusalem and its temple; the city of Jerusalem is transformed. John's audience is aware that the former city of Jerusalem was destroyed in 70 CE, but he does not dwell on that. His interests lie elsewhere. Just as the heavens, the earth, and the sea pass away to allow for the new creation, John does not portray a city made of bricks and mortar, but a spiritual reality, which will manifest itself in a communion between God and humankind (see 21:3-4).

In 21:2 the woman is described as the "bride" (Greek: *nymphē*), but her identity with "the woman" of chapters 12 and 17 will be made clear, when the "bride" is further described in her description in 22:9 as "the woman" (Greek: *hē gunē*). The potential of the woman, lost in 12:1-6, is now restored because of the death and resurrection of Jesus. The repulsive wickedness of the portrait of the woman mounted on the beast, slaying Israel's holy ones in 17:1-6, is reversed. Humankind regains its potential because of the death and resurrection of Jesus.

God speaks from the throne and describes a new situation, so opposed to the violence and wickedness that determined the world while Satan and his agents ruled (e.g., 17:1-6). Despite its transformation from a worldly to a spiritual reality, the new creation is not an "otherworldly" presence of God to the human situation. Continuing to use marital language associated with the nuptial union, the voice announces that God will set up his tent among human beings. God will become part of the human story. The oft-repeated Old Testament promise: "I will be their God and they shall be my people" (Jer 32:38; Ezek 37:27. See also Gen 17:8; Exod 29:45; Lev 26:45; Ezek 14:11; Zech 8:8) is strengthened by the use of a verb that repeats the idea of setting up a tent among his people: "He will dwell with them; they will be his peoples" (v. 3ab). The sufferings that have been part of the ambiguity of Israel's history, named "the first things" (vv. 4d), are recognized: tears, death, mourning, crying, and pain (v. 4abc).

The list of death, mourning, crying, and pain that are a characteristic of the "first things" recalls the consequences of the fall recorded in Genesis 3:14-19. But with the establishment of the New Jerusalem, that situation has disappeared. The tears will be wiped away; death is overcome; mourning, crying, and pain are no more. Suffering, death, and ambiguity have been replaced by a nuptial union with God who has overcome all evil and dwells "among mortals" through the death and resurrection of Jesus Christ. The "first things," the period that marked the era from the fall to the coming of Jesus Christ, the Lamb, the Son of Man, have passed away. The new creation is firmly located among men and women.

The voice from the throne speaks again, reinforcing what has already been said: what is now available to those who are saved in this final act of judgment is totally new. God is the agent of this newness, but it has been communicated through Jesus Christ, the rider of the white horse who is called "Faithful and True," clothed in a robe dipped in blood, the Word of God, King of kings and Lord of lords (19:11-16). The acclamation announcing that the saving event of the death and resurrection of Jesus had been accomplished, as the seventh bowl was poured out, is repeated: "It is done!" (v. 6a. See 16:17). Recalling the absolute lordship of God, already proclaimed in the prologue (see 1:8), the voice reminds the audience that throughout the whole of human history, through the era of Israel, and the "new" that has now begun, God has always been God: "I am the Alpha and the Omega, the beginning and the end" (v. 6b). Whatever the vicissitudes of humankind's relationship to God, nothing alters God's absolute lordship across the whole of sacred history, in both Israel and the Christian community.

John summons his audience to recognize that there is a source of life for them, as they live in the challenging Greco-Roman world. John makes it clear that other choices are possible. God may have definitively overcome Satan, the beast, and the false prophet, and destroyed all their cohorts (19:20-21; 21:10). But they still "live" in the fiery lake, and the choice of evil is still available. The possibility of sin still exists. What is said in v. 8, addressed directly to John's audience living in the Greco-Roman world, is clear indication that the battles reported in 19:7-21 and 20:7-10 are *not* the end of all wickedness. Christian life amid the ambiguities of the Greco-Roman world goes on (see also 16:9, 11, 21). Many will continue to be tempted into cowardice, faithlessness, pollution through participation in pagan cultic activities, murder, immoral lifestyles, idolatry of false gods, and lies.

Cowardice and faithlessness are the *antithesis* of the models of Israel's saints, who gave their lives out of faithfulness to the Law and the acceptance of the messianic promises. John's Christians are blessed to live in the messianic "new" era, but cowardice in the face of the powerful currents of Greco-Roman thought and practice inevitably leads to faithlessness and its consequences. Although they do not have to suffer martyrdom to participate in the new life made available by the death and resurrection of Jesus, John's audience must demonstrate the courage, faithfulness, and resistance that marked the lives and deaths of Israel's saints as they now live the in-between-time of the New Jerusalem. Resistance to the powers of evil is still required.

# THURSDAY

## *The New Jerusalem (21:9-21)*

In 21:1-2 the New Jerusalem was described as the bride. In 21:9 she is the wife (Greek: *hē gunē*) of the Lamb. The angel transports John, now "in the spirit," to a great high mountain. He establishes a striking contrast between his words that open the vision of the destruction of 17:1–19:10 and the subsequent vision of consequences of the new creation in 21:9–22:5. In 17:3 he reported: "He carried me away in the spirit into a wilderness, and I saw a woman on a scarlet beast." The same action, with different consequences, takes place in 21:10: "In the spirit he carried me away to a great, high mountain and showed me the holy city Jerusalem coming down out of heaven from God." A further significant contrast between the earlier appearances of the woman is present. The woman clothed with the sun fell from heaven into the ambiguity of the desert (12:6, 14). As a prostitute to the beast, she was in the desert (17:3). The final appearance of "the woman" is "on a great, high mountain" (21:10). The desert no longer plays a role because the New Jerusalem, like Mount Zion, is on a mountain.

The mountain is a well-used biblical image of a place *on earth* where God establishes contact with human beings (see, for example, Exod 19:3-23; Deut 34:1-4; Matt 5:1; 17:1; 28:16). The tradition of an encounter with God on a mountain, whatever its usage in variations based on the original gift of the Law at Sinai, is not concerned with ascensions *into heaven*, but about the formation and nourishment of a people of God *on earth.* The heavenly Jerusalem is *"from* God." John, carried to the mountain in the spirit, beholds the descent of the heavenly "holy city Jerusalem" to take up its location as a place of encounter between God and humankind on the great, high mountain, *on earth.*

The description of the city begins with an affirmation that it contains the "glory of God," and a brilliant radiance that can only be expressed in a comparative fashion: "like a very rare jewel." Nothing created can be used as an exact description of the glory of God that dwells in the city. These "comparatives" indicate to the audience that the New Jerusalem, experienced in the lived reality of a Christian community, is a spiritual experience, beyond precise measurement and description. The expression "the glory of God" has a long biblical history, with its beginnings in the revelation of God on Sinai. It is *always* associated with the visible presence of the divine *within human history and experience.*[7] What that meant in real terms for John's audience is not indicated with clarity, although the promises made to the churches certainly have this intent (see 2:7, 11, 17, 27-28; 3:5-6, 12, 21). Such experiences in the church depended upon their sharing a way of life made possible by the death and resurrection of Jesus, so frequently and loudly proclaimed from the beginning to the end of Revelation.

John continues to compare the luminous nature of the *doxa* of God by indicating an example of a "very rare jewel": "like jasper, clear as crystal" (v. 11b). This is the beginning of a practice that he expands further in his description of the city: "the wall is built of jasper, while the city is pure gold, clear as glass" (v. 18). It continues into the descriptions of the foundations of the walls of the city (vv. 19-20: jasper, sapphire, agate,

---

[7] See Francis J. Moloney, *Belief in the Word. Reading John 1–4* (Minneapolis: Fortress, 1993), 55–57. See p. 56: "The expression is used to speak of a presence that can be seen, heard, felt, or experienced by the people themselves, or by individuals."

emerald, onyx, carnelian, beryl, topaz, chrysoprase, jacinth, and amethyst), its twelve gates (v. 21a: pearls), and its street (v. 21b: pure gold). What these precious stones represent, and even what some of them are, is impossible to recognize with precision. John creates an image of a heavenly Jerusalem filled with the glory of God and built with brilliant, crystal clear stones. The description opens with a description of the city as "pure gold, clear as glass" (v. 18), and closes with an inclusion, describing the street of the city as "pure gold, transparent as glass" (v. 21). Gold is neither clear as glass, nor transparent, but John's point is made by means of hyperbole. All the elements used to construct the hyperbole are humanly recognizable examples of luminous beauty. The filth and shame of the city destroyed in 17:1–19:10 have been replaced in the new creation (see 21:1-8) with a New Jerusalem: God's splendid and spectacular dwelling place on earth (21:12-17). All the trappings of wealth and success that were the result of corrupt human activity, on land and sea, have been destroyed. They have been replaced by God-given treasures.

The remaining feature of the description of the heavenly Jerusalem is the result of the measuring activity of the angel. Taking his cue from the lengthy description of the renewed temple found in Ezekiel 40–42, the structure of the heavenly Jerusalem is described in vv. 12-17. With a golden rod, he measures the city, its gates, and its walls (see Ezek 40:5). In Revelation 11:1 the temple, the altar, and the worshippers were measured with an ordinary reed. But as this is no ordinary city, it requires a rod made of pure gold. Every aspect of what is measured in John's city from above is a multiple of the number "twelve." Secondly, although not specifically mentioned in 21:9-21, an audience aware of the promises of Ezekiel 40–42 and its focus upon the details of the restored Jerusalem temple is also aware that there is no temple in the city.

The great high wall that surrounds the city has twelve gates, and twelve angels stand at the gates, like the ever-watchful

sentinels of Isaiah (see Isa 62:6). Inscribed on the gates are
the names of the twelve tribes of the Israelites (v. 12). The city
has four walls, and each wall (east, north, south, and west) has
three gates. There are thus twelve gates (v. 13. See v. 12). The
city stands four-square, equidistant in length, width, and height.
Its measurement is twelve thousand stadia. The height of the
wall is also a multiple of twelve: 144 cubits, as measured by
the angel (v. 17). For John the number "twelve" serves as a
number, not only of totality but also of perfection. Secondly,
and crucially, the key to the use of the "twelve" is the historical
and theological continuation between God's chosen people:
"the names of the twelve tribes of the Israelites" (v. 12) and
the new community of God, the Christian church founded
upon "the names of the twelve apostles of the Lamb" (v. 14).
As God chose the twelve tribes of Israel, a new people of God
is founded upon the twelve apostles of the Lamb, the result
of the death and resurrection of Jesus.

Immediately following the description of the restored Jerusalem in Ezekiel 40–42, "the glory of the Lord" enters and fills
the temple (Ezek 43:1-4. See Rev 21:11). A voice comes out
of the temple, instructing Ezekiel: "Son of man, this is the place
of my throne and the place for the soles of my feet, where I
will reside among the people of Israel forever. The house of
Israel will no more defile my holy name" (Ezek 43:7 AT). John's
vision of the heavenly Jerusalem, the bride of the Lamb, the
dwelling place of the glory of God, is constructed with gates
inscribed with the names of the twelve tribes of Israel, resting
upon foundations bearing the names of the twelve apostles
of the Lamb. Its advent from God is the result of God's new
creation (Rev 21:1-8). John sees the bride adorned for her
spouse (21:2). Then, in a fashion that parallels Ezekiel's experience in Ezekiel 43:1-7, a loud voice from the throne cried out:
"See the home of God is among mortals. He will dwell with
them . . . and God himself will be with them" (21:3). Looking
back to his constant source of inspiration, the Hebrew Bible,
John tells his audience of a new place, where God dwells

among his people, inscribed with the names of the twelve tribes of Israel and founded upon the names of the twelve apostles of the Lamb (Ezek 43:7; Rev 21:3, 11, 12b, 14b).

## Dwelling in the New Jerusalem (21:22-27)

Reflecting the description of the New Jerusalem in vv. 9-21, where no temple was mentioned, John states that he saw no temple in the city (v. 22). In the New Jerusalem there is no need for a temple and its cultic activities because God and the Lamb dwell in the city. It is not as if a temple has been destroyed and replaced. Once God and the Lamb are enthroned in the city, the whole city becomes the place where the believer encounters God. Making a further connection with vv. 9-21, again dependent upon Isaiah 60, John points out that the city has no need for the natural sources of light, the sun by day and the moon by night, because the glory of God dwells there (see v. 11), and the lamp that carries God's light is the Lamb whose death and resurrection have transformed human history (v. 23). John's vision of the New Jerusalem (vv. 9-21), and his affirmation that the presence of God and the Lamb eliminates all need for a temple, has been stated in the present tense. The new creation, initiated by the death and resurrection has provided a new place, a New Jerusalem, where God and his Christ dwell among us.

From this point on, down to the final affirmation of v. 27, every verb is in the future tense. The presence of God's glory and the light born by the Lamb reach beyond John's immediate audience; they are to become universally available. The city will never be shut, and an everlasting day will be available, as night will never descend (v. 25). Another reversal of the darkness that surrounded the destruction of Jerusalem in 17:1–19:10 marks the entry of "the nations" and "the kings of the earth" into the New Jerusalem, and the presence of God and the Lamb. Judged as participants in the satanic agenda that generated the destruction of Jerusalem, "the nations" (see 17:15; 18:3,

23) and "the kings of the earth" (see 17:2, 9, 12 [twice], 14; 18:3, 9) are given a surprisingly positive evaluation in v. 24. John seems to accept that not all have committed themselves to the satanic agenda and will thus have entry to the new dwelling place of God and God's people. The nations will enter the holy city and will walk by its light.

Equally surprising is John's further recognition that there are "kings of this earth" that possess a "glory" that they will bring with them into the New Jerusalem. This glory cannot be compared to the glory of God of vv. 11 and 23, but there must be some "kings of the earth" who have resisted the seduction of Satan and his agents. Possessing a reflected glory they *will enter* the New Jerusalem. The same future is to be granted to an unidentified plural group who will bring "the glory and honor of the nations." Not all "the nations" and not all "the kings of the earth" are destroyed (as in 17:1–19:10). Some will dwell in the New Jerusalem (21:22-27).

Although not a major feature of John's book of Revelation, members of John's audience sense that they share in the early church's call to mission that began with the death and resurrection of Jesus. For John, perhaps influenced by Isaiah 60:6-9, this mission involved entry into the New Jerusalem. Indeed, for the Christians in Asia this is an encouraging message. Most likely a majority non-Jewish group of early believers, they could identify themselves as the fruits of the early church's missionary agenda. Indeed, John is on the island of Patmos because of his missionary zeal for them (1:9).

This interpretation of vv. 24-26 is enhanced by the negative assessment of the one who will not enter the city (v. 27). Recalling the ongoing existence of failures that would lead to the second death in 21:8 (see also 22:3a, 11, 15), John insists that the unclean will never enter the New Jerusalem: those who practice abomination or falsehood (v. 27). Only those whose names are written in the Lamb's book of life will be admitted. Abomination, the practice of idol worship, so often condemned by John, or falsehood, pretending to be what one was not, a failure of all the churches of Asia (2:1–3:22), would no doubt have been ongoing temptations for John's audience. John challenges them to live as the visible fruits of the death and resurrection of Jesus within the powerful and attractive context of a Greco-Roman world, already mirrored in the participation of Israel's martyrs, especially during the time of Antiochus IV, in the saving effects of the Lamb, slain before the foundation of the world (13:8).

# FRIDAY

## *Life and light (22:1-5)*

Revelation 22:1-5, strongly influenced by the immediately preceding passage (21:22-27), is based upon the vision of Ezekiel 47:1-12 but marked by the now-familiar reshaping of the earlier prophet's vision by the prophet John. It is his final vision. In the New Jerusalem, God and the Lamb are the temple: the presence of the divine light. Thus, the source of "the river of the water of life" is the throne of God and of the Lamb (Rev 22:1. See Ezek 47:1). Associated with God and the Lamb as the unique sources of light described in 21:23, the flowing water in the river is "bright as crystal." For Ezekiel the water that flows from the temple leaves the city of Jerusalem via the south gate, and heads, ever deepening, to nourish the desert regions of the Arabah (see Ezek 47:2, 8). For John the water flows through the "middle of the street" of the city (Rev 22:2. See 21:21). A golden street, clear as glass (21:21), carries the life-giving water throughout the city. Ezekiel 47:12 provides the background for the theme of the nourishment that the living water of the river brings to the plant life, but for John there is only one tree: the tree of life (Rev 22:2). As in Ezekiel 47:12, the fruit provides nourishment and the leaves bring healing. However, the tree of life in the New Jerusalem bears fruit twelve times a year, once every month. The river of life and its fruit-bearing tree are always present. The missionary theme returns fleetingly as the healing brought by the leaves of the tree is directed to "the nations" (see 21:24, 26).

These themes, however, expressed so succinctly in 22:1-2, enable John to take his audience back to the innocent origins of humankind. Genesis 2:10-14 describes the origin of all the waters of the earth as "a river [that] flows out of Eden" (Gen 2:10). The symbol of life-giving water, coming from humankind's location in Eden and spreading across the earth, links the river flowing from the throne of God and the Lamb to the situation before the fall. Also crucial to the narrative in Genesis at this point is "the tree of life" in the middle of the garden (v. 9). Imaginatively combining the witness of Genesis and Ezekiel, John places "the tree of life" beside the river, providing the universal enjoyment of its fruits (see also Ezek 14:7, 12). In this way, his allusion to Ezekiel draws the audience back to a recognition of the New Jerusalem as a restoration of the innocent origins of humankind.

The New Jerusalem is the place where God and the Lamb are present. From them flow life and healing, restoring humankind to its full potential. Again, however, John issues a warning: "Nothing accursed will be found there any more" (Rev 22:3a). This affirmation is a clear reference to the city filled with sins of all kinds, the former Jerusalem that has been destroyed as a consequence of the death and resurrection of Jesus in the narrative of 17:1–19:10. This situation does not exist "any more." Healing and forgiveness are available through contact with the leaves that grow from the living water flowing from the throne of God and the Lamb; but those who reject what the death and resurrection have made available in the New Jerusalem are to be excluded. A subtle hint of the ongoing presence of the New Jerusalem as the lordship and dwelling place (the throne) of God and the Lamb is found in the return to verbs that are in the future tense. Nothing accursed "will be found there any more." What was once will be no more. Now, only servants "will worship" God. John's opening description of the community to which he addressed this document is recalled: because of Jesus' death and resurrection they are a kingdom of priests, serving the God and Father of Jesus Christ, the firstborn from the dead (see 1:5-6).

These servants and priests will be uniquely blessed: "[T]hey will see his face, and his name will be on their foreheads" (v. 4a). A well-known biblical tradition insists that no one can see the face of God (see Exod 33:20-23) has been reversed. The condemnation of those who bore the mark of the beast (see 13:1, 17; 17:3, 5) has been reversed by the servants of God and the Lamb who dwell in the New Jerusalem (see also 7:3). They not only bear the mark of God, but they bear his name upon their foreheads (22:4b). As those who bore the mark of the beast belonged to him, those who bear the name of God and the Lamb belong to the new order established by the death and resurrection of Jesus.

The theme of light, so central to 21:22-27 and 22:1-5 (see 21:23-26; 22:1), returns in John's final statement about the New Jerusalem. All those who dwell there will have no more night or need of a lamp or the sun. "For the Lord God will shine light upon them" (v. 5a AT. See 21:22-27). In that light, as part of a kingdom, priests serving the God and Father of Jesus Christ, "the faithful witness, the firstborn of the dead, and the ruler of the kings of the earth" (1:5-6), will reign forever (22:5b).

To tell Christians that they will reign forever and ever has never meant that they would avoid the constraints of history. No early Christian author tells his audience that they will never experience physical death. This was clearly one of the issues that created what is most likely our earliest Christian document, 1 Thessalonians. But Paul disabuses the Thessalonian Christians of any such idea (see 1 Thess 4:13–5:11). The promise of eternal life has always been made to Christians who commit themselves to belief in the saving effects of Jesus' death and resurrection and strive to live a lifestyle that manifests that commitment. For John, all people must face death (see Rev 20:6). In due course all people, except of those who were slain for their adherence to the Law and their acceptance of the messianic promises, will be "judged according to what they had done" (20:13).

There are several important contacts between the "promises to the victor" in the letters to the seven churches across 2:1–3:22, and the concluding pages of Revelation, dedicated to the establishment and description of the New Jerusalem (21:1–22:5). The seven letters are directed to the church itself, potentially the new community of God, but stumbling in the face of the challenges of their surrounding Greco-Roman world. The New Jerusalem is also "the church itself," the new community of God with its potential realized. *Ephesus* was promised that the victor would taste the fruits of the tree of life in the paradise of God (2:2). This promise is fulfilled in the tree of life, found in the *New Jerusalem* (22:2). The Christians in *Smyrna* were promised that they would not be struck by the "second death" (2:11), an experience that is guaranteed for those martyrs of Israel (20:6). But such "death" will be the destiny of all who are unfaithful in the *New Jerusalem* (20:14; 21:8). The believers in *Pergamum* were promised a white stone (2:17), fulfilled in the many brilliant stones used to describe the *New Jerusalem* in 21:18-21. The promise made to *Thyatira* that it would be given authority over the nations and the morning star (2:27-28) is fulfilled in the reign of a thousand years of Israel's saints (20:4-6), and their encounter with the Lamb in the *New Jerusalem* (21:22-23), described in 22:16 as "the bright morning star." The promise is made to those in *Sardis* who are wearing white garments that their names will not be canceled from the book of life (3:5). That promise is realized in the *New Jerusalem* (20:12). A promise that captures much of the message of 21:9–22:5 is made to the faithful in *Philadelphia*: "I will make you a pillar in the temple of my God; you will never go out of it. I will write on you the name of my God, and the name of the city of my God the *new Jerusalem* that comes down from my God out of heaven, and my own new name" (3:12, emphasis added). These promises become a reality in the New Jerusalem in 21:10,

22-27, and 22:4. Finally, the promise to the faithful in Laodicea that they would sit down on Christ's throne, is fulfilled in the *New Jerusalem* in 22:1-2 (see 3:20).

As well as the promises to the victors in the seven letters, the one like a Son of Man also issues threats: to remove the candelabra (2:5), to destroy the idolatry of prostitution to political authority (2:14, 20-23), to cancel their name from the book of life (3:5). The final harsh letter to Laodicea issues final warnings that are precise allusions to the destruction of Babylon/Jerusalem in chapter 18 (see 3:14-17 and 18:9-21). These threats raise the possibility that a chosen people might betray its call to follow the Lamb wherever he goes (see 14:4).

John's literary and theological intentions are clear: the church (the "seven") is the spiritual New Jerusalem, the fulfillment of the promises of the Law and the prophets, through the death and resurrection of Jesus. Those who dwell in the Christian community, the New Jerusalem, surrounded by the ambiguous glitter of the Greco-Roman world, are assured that whatever challenges the present and the future may hold, because the Lamb has been slain and is once again standing (see 5:6), they "will reign forever and ever" (22:5).

# CHAPTER TEN

## *Fifth Week of Easter: Saturday*

### Making Sense of Revelation 22:6-21

### *"Worship God!" (22:6-9)*

Recalling the very first verse of the book, John reminds his audience that "the Lord, the God of the spirits and of the prophets" show what must take place quickly (v. 6b. See 1:1).[1] John informs his audience, as he opens and closes his book (1:1; 22:6), that the events communicated through the angels and the prophets cannot be delayed by any opposing force. It "must happen." The narrative of Revelation 1:1–22:5 has told the story, communicated by angels and the prophet John, of the Christological interpretation of the Law and the prophets. These events had to happen speedily, and they did, as one symbolic representation of Jesus' death and resurrection and its consequences tumbled upon one another in breathtaking fashion.

Without any introduction, the speaker changes. The voice of Jesus Christ announces, in the first person: "See, I am coming quickly!" (AT). The New Jerusalem has been established (21:9–22:5). The saving effects of the crucified and risen Christ have been present in history from its foundation (see 13:8) and

---

[1] The return to themes from the prologue of 1:1-8 in 22:6 is one of several indications that 22:6-21 forms the epilogue of the book of Revelation.

will be present till the end (see 1:8; 22:13). The holy ones of Israel already participate in the reign of the crucified and risen Christ (see, especially, 20:1-6). But a new era of God's life-giving presence has begun with the death and resurrection of Jesus, and the establishment of the Christian community, the New Jerusalem. Jesus' unannounced entry into the narrative looks back across that story and points the members of the Christian community to a final coming.

The sudden and unexpected inbreak of the voice of Jesus Christ illustrates the meaning of "quickly": "See, I come unexpectedly" (v. 7 AT). Jesus is not warning of an *imminent* final coming (its "timing"), but that when it comes, it will come *quickly* and *unexpectedly* (its "nature"). This is the point of the penultimate "beatitude" of Revelation: "Blessed is the one who keeps the words of the authoritative witness to the divine purpose of this book" (AT). Between the "now" of their experience of life given by the crucified and risen Lamb (5:6) that John has shared in his writing, and the "not yet" of the eventual second coming of Jesus Christ (22:20), Christians are living an in-between-time. Across that time, the length of which is unknown to John and to his audience, they must keep the words of the interpretation of "this book."

Which book? This is a critical question, given the eightfold occurrence of expressions associated with "this book" in the epilogue (vv. 6, 7, 9, 10, 18 [twice], 19 [twice]). Throughout Revelation, John has addressed believing Christians. He told them the story of their foundation upon Israel, and the richly rewarded endurance of the saints of that era. The New Jerusalem does not replace the former Jerusalem. John has used angels and prophets to tell the message of Israel's "book," focusing particularly upon the role of the pre-Christian slain witnesses to God and Jesus Christ. They held fast to the Law and accepted the messianic proclamation of the prophets (see 1:2, 9; 6:9; 12:17; 19:10; 20:4). They already enjoy their reign with God and the Lamb. By their deaths they already participate in the perennial presence of Jesus' saving death and resurrection (see especially 20:1-6).

John has written *his* book to provide access to the interpretation of *their* book. For John the crucially important "book" is the one that contains the word of God in the Law and the prophets (see vv. 18-19). Without the message of Israel's "book," there would be no Christian era and no reason for writing Revelation. A "history of salvation" lies behind John's reading of Israel's Scriptures. John's prophetic work indicates to early Christians that they now have access to life and light because of the death and resurrection of Jesus, and the Christian era that flows from that event. Blessed is the one "takes to heart" these authoritative interpretations of the divine purpose (v. 7b AT). They dwell in the New Jerusalem (22:1-5).

John, who saw and heard these things, returns in v. 8a. After the sudden intervention of the voice of Jesus in v. 7, the link with the response of John to the visions of the destruction of Jerusalem in 19:10-11 is resumed in 22:8b-9. As in 19:10, John prostrates himself to worship the angel (22:8b) but is firmly instructed that such worship is out of place (22:9). The mediating angel, John, the mediating prophet, all mediating Christian prophets ("your comrades the prophets"), and all those dwelling in the New Jerusalem who take to heart the words of this book form a single community committed to a single responsibility: "Worship God!" (v. 9c). But there is narrative progression between 19:10 and 22:9, with the addition of the Christian community to the list of witnesses. In 22:9 the witness to Jesus is now available to all who dwell in the New Jerusalem, established in and through the death and resurrection of Jesus. Added to the *witnesses* of 19:10 are the *recipients of that witness*: all those who take to heart the words of this book. All members of the church, the Christian community (angels, authoritative interpreters of the divine purpose, witnesses, and recipients of that witness), are called to worship God (22:10), in the light of what John has revealed to them.

# SATURDAY

### *"Come!" (22:10-17)*[2]

A focus upon "the interpretation of the words of this book" continues in v. 10. The words are not to be sealed up, because God's opportune time is at hand. The Greek expression *kairos*, taken from the apostolic preaching (see, for example, Mark 1:15; 13:33; Matt 26:18; Luke 12:56; 18:30; 19:44; 20:10; 21:8, 24, 36. See also Mark 11:13; 12:2; Matt 21:41), indicates the "divine opportunity" of God's visitation in and through the presence, death, and resurrection of Jesus. John instructs that "this book" of the revelation of Jesus Christ (1:1) must never again be sealed. John's audience, Christian believers in the Greco-Roman world, have been informed by John's unraveling of "this book" that they are living the "divine opportunity" of the New Jerusalem (21:9–22:5). However, they live it in a society that does not share their belief in the Lamb's unsealing of the divine story of the Lamb, slain from before the foundation of the world (13:8), whose death and resurrection produced the New Jerusalem.

The experience of the coexistence of a Christian community and a world that does not share their beliefs and values has been mentioned regularly, from the problems that afflicted the churches to the lack of repentance and the ongoing reality of wickedness in the face of God's saving action (see 2:1–3:22; 16:8-9, 11, 21; 18:4; 21:8, 27; 22:3). It is eloquently stated in v. 11: "Let the evildoer still do evil, and the filthy still be filthy, and the righteous still do right, and the holy still be holy." It will be restated in v. 15. This affirmation describes the historical situation of believers struggling to maintain their belief and righteousness in an evil and filthy world.[3] There is no sign of

---

[2] Revelation 22:12-14, 16-17, 20 provides the second reading in the Liturgy of the Word for the Seventh Sunday of Easter in Year C.

[3] Early Christians regarded many of the practices of the Greco-Roman world as filthy and evil. Early Christianity's concerns with the Greco-Roman world were not primarily about its morality. That was only part of a broader

an imminent end to human history, with its conflicts and ambiguities. With "this book" in hand, the members of the community are made aware that God is on their side. For John, his visions and prophecies of the three "sevens" and the three consequences of the death and resurrection of Jesus (17:1–21:8) unravel *what was promised in Israel's Sacred Scriptures*.

The voice of Jesus again interrupts: "I am coming quickly" (v. 12a AT. See v. 7a). His second pronouncement looks back to what the angel has described as "the second death" (see 20:6, 14). At that time "all were judged according to what they had done" (20:13). Jesus' final coming will be accompanied with a judgment where humankind will be measured "according to everyone's work" (22:12). There will be an end of all time, and it will bring its own judgment. The audience is told that when this judgment comes, it will come quickly. Set between two indications of the wickedness that surround the everyday lived experience of the audience (see vv. 11 and 15), Jesus announces that judgment belongs to him, and it will be both positive and negative. Jesus is the one who will allocate the respective reward. "My reward is with me."

For the moment, Christians are asked by Jesus to put their trust in him who joins his Father's lordship over the whole of creation and history: "I am the Alpha and the Omega, the first and the last, the beginning and the end" (v. 13. See 1:8). Judgment will be made upon the good (vv. 7b, 14) and upon the wicked (vv. 11 and 15) in due course. They will be judged according to their works (v. 12b. See 20:13).

After Jesus' self-revelatory pronouncements of vv. 12-13 only the voice of Jesus is heard until John's response and closing salutation to his audience in vv. 20b-21. The ambiguous situation of the audience returns in vv. 14-17. Recalling the privileged situation of those who have been saved, Jesus Christ issues the final beatitude of Revelation, blessing the

---

complex of unacceptable religious and structural practices, especially in the empire. See Rodney Stark, *The Rise of Christianity. A Sociologist Reconsiders History* (Princeton, NJ: Princeton University Press, 1996).

dwellers in the New Jerusalem. They have a right to the tree of life (see 22:2) and access to the God-given city through its gates (see 21:12-13, 21, 25-27).

But outside the city, wickedness continues. The wicked are generically described as "dogs" (see Ps 22:16; 1 Sam 24:14; Matt 7:6; 15:26; Phil 3:2; 2 Pet 2:22), and the nature of their sinfulness is listed: sorcerers, fornicators, idolaters, and those who love and practice falsehood (v. 15). Much of the wickedness accredited to the "dogs" outside the city has been described as present in the seven churches in 2:1–3:22 (see 2:15 [sorcery?]; 2:14, 20 [fornication]; 2:14, 20 [idolaters]; 2:2, 14, 23-24; 3:2-3, 9, 16-17 [falsehood]). As the work comes to an end, the "ideal" of the New Jerusalem (21:9–22:5) has been presented to an imperfect church (2:1–3:22). A late-first-century Christian Church is being asked to take stock of itself. Where does it belong: in the New Jerusalem generated by the death and resurrection of Jesus (v. 14), or outside the holy city, selling itself out to the practices of the Greco-Roman world in which they live their day-to-day lives (v. 15)?

The authority of Jesus lies behind this challenge. What has been communicated from the angels, through the reported visionary experiences of John, has its origins in Jesus. Almost everything in the narrative has been mediated through angels and the telling of prophetic signs. Mediation has come to an end: "It is I, Jesus" (v. 16a). This figure is already known to the audience as the Messiah, "the root and descendent of David" (see 5:5). Recalling a promise made to the community in Thyatira, he is further described as "the bright morning star" (v. 16b. See 2:28. See also 2 Pet 1:19). On the basis of his messianic authority Jesus informs the audience that he is one with the Spirit of God and the bride of the Lamb, the Spirit-filled Christian community, as he issues his command: "Come" (v. 17a)!

The earlier description of those "inside" (v. 14) and those "outside" (v. 15) must be kept in mind. Living in a world marked by ambiguity, and a Christian community also marked by ambiguity (see 2:1–3:22), the believer is summoned to enter the New Jerusalem. This is a call to enter the Christian community, to be dressed in white, made clean by the blood of the Lamb (see, for example, 7:9-17). But the call to "enter" is not only issued by Jesus; it is a community responsibility. As the messianic Jesus calls people to the city, so also everyone who hears Jesus' invitation is asked, in her or his own turn, to call to those "outside" to "come" inside (v. 17b). However succinct, v. 17b is part of the awareness of the missionary responsibility of the earliest church. What Jesus does, so does the Christian disciple (see, for example, Mark 3:13-15; 6:7-13; John 13:34-35; Phil 1:27–2:11; 1 John 2:6).

Closing this section of Revelation 22:6-17, Jesus returns to his promise (see 22:1), that those who wish to satisfy their thirst will receive the gift of the water of life (22:17c). Those who "come," enter the New Jerusalem and receive the water of life from Jesus, "the bright morning star." As the angel promised in the final words of his description of the New Jerusalem: "The Lord God will be their light, and they will reign forever and ever" (22:5. See 21:23-24).

## Warning, promise, and response (22:18-21)

The words of Jesus continue in the severe warning of vv. 18-19, addressed to all who hear the words of "this book" (18a). Jesus warns that nothing is to be added to the words of "this book" (v. 18) and nothing is to be taken away (v. 19). The prohibition is linked to a punishment that matches the offense. The person who "adds" will have the plagues described in "this book" added to their lives (v. 18b. See 15:1–16:21: the plagues that follow the pouring out of the seven bowls, all of which recapitulate the plagues of the exodus). Whoever "takes away" will have the blessings of the New Jerusalem described in this book (see 21:9–22:5: a share in the tree of life and in the holy city, all of which recapitulates the promises of Genesis and Ezekiel) taken away (v. 19). In terms of the theology of Revelation, the former group will not benefit from the saving action of the Lamb (see 16:10-21), and the latter will remain outside God's gift of the holy city (21:27). They will dwell among the "dogs" (see 22:15).

Most suggest that John asks that their lives match the message of his book, regarding his word as having the same authority as the word of Jesus, the Word of God. This can hardly be the case, as John has made it clear on two occasions that he enjoys no such superior authority. Like the revealing angel and the prophetic brotherhood, he is a servant of the one true God (see 19:10a; 22:9). In bearing witness to Jesus, they exercise their ministry as authoritative interpreters of the divine purpose (see 19:10b; 22:9). The book that Jesus insists must not be altered in any way (vv. 18-19) is the Sacred Scriptures of Israel. They tell the story of God's care for humankind with his Law, and they are filled with the messianic promises of the prophets. John's "book" has recourse to Israel's Sacred Scriptures at every turn.

No doubt he regarded his own work as giving vision and direction to the Christian church in Asia at the end of the first century. But it was not his book that could bear no alteration. The articulation of God's design belongs only to the Sacred Scriptures of Israel. John's work makes that clear. His audience received his book attentively. Despite its troubled history, especially in the East, John's book was passed from generation to generation, and eventually found a place in the Christian canon. The book that John's words impregnate with Christological significance, drawing from it at every turn, is the Sacred Scripture of Israel. That "book" must not be added to or taken from, for the word of God stands forever (see Isa 40:8).

John closes with a proclamation and a response that may reflect a liturgical event.[4] Jesus, the one who has guaranteed

----

[4] Many rightly identify liturgical and Eucharistic background across the book of Revelation. Especially rich in this regard are the commentaries of Pierre Prigent, *Commentary on the Apocalypse of St. John*, trans. Wendy Pradels (Tübingen: Mohr Siebeck, 2001), and Boxall, *Revelation,* Black's New Testament Commentaries (London: A. & C. Black, 2006).

all that has been told to this point, proclaims: "Surely, I am coming quickly" (v. 20a AT). In 22:6-21 the early Christian message of the return of Jesus has been stated three times (vv. 7, 12, 20a). Jesus' final proclamation of his second coming is prefaced with a comforting "surely." Despite the earlier witnesses of 1 Thessalonians and 1 Corinthians (e.g., 1 Thess 4:13–5:11; 1 Cor 7:25-31, Mark 9:1), the eager expectation of an imminent end-time has eased by the end of the first century. Jesus insists *that* he will come, and that he will come quickly. But *when and how* that will happen remains unknown (see Mark 13:32).

The adequate Christian antiphonal response to Jesus' affirmation is acceptance. Making use of an acclamation that was apparently widespread in the early church (see 1 Cor 16:22), John responds: "Amen." So be it! "Come, Lord Jesus!" (v. 20b). But a long journey through history may lie ahead. John does not know, but he again adopts a formula widely used by the writers of New Testament letters to close with a prayer for his fellow Christians (see Col 4:18; 1 Tim 6:21; 2 Tim 4:22b; Titus 3:15; Heb 13:25). He asks that the grace of the Lord Jesus may accompany them along their journey into the future, challenged on every side in a Greco-Roman world, but comforted by the fact that they dwell in the New Jerusalem, made possible by the death and resurrection of Jesus. They do not have to wait for an imminent eschatological climax to all history for a victory that gives light and life (see 22:1-5). God, through the death and resurrection of the Lamb, has established a blessed era that is experienced and witnessed to in their day-to-day lives, enjoying the gift of light and life, available in the New Jerusalem. God has transformed the human story, while continuing his perennial saving presence, in and through the death and resurrection of the Lamb, Jesus Christ. Amen.

# Appendix

The recognition that the book of Revelation is an Easter book is one of the main factors that has determined its use in the Roman liturgy. I offer the following indications of its regular appearances in the liturgy to direct an interested reader to the relevant sections of the commentary for some guidance. Passages from Revelation that appear regularly, or on important liturgical celebrations, are indicated by changing the typeface for the relevant commentary and the accompanying explanatory footnote. The intense focus upon proclamation of texts from the book of Revelation for Easter celebrations is a powerful reminder of the central role the death and resurrection of Jesus Christ plays in John's argument: *lex orandi lex credendi.* The way the church prays reflects what the church believes.

## *Liturgy of the Hours*

There is a single-minded focus upon the use of four exultant resurrection texts in the choice of canticles for celebrations of Evening Prayer:

1. A collection of texts from the heavenly encounter, praising God the Creator and the Lamb as Savior that introduces the opening of the seven seals: Revelation 4:11; 5:9, 10, 12.

2. The song of triumph that marks the blowing of the seventh trumpet, linked with a song honoring the redeemed saints: Revelation 11:17-18; 12:10b-12a.

3. The song of Moses and the song of the Lamb, part of the heavenly encounter that opens the pouring out of the seven bowls: Revelation 15:3-4.

4. The rejoicing in heaven that follows the victory of the Lamb: Revelation 19:1-2, 5-7.

Praise of God the Creator (4:11), and of the Lamb, the one who redeemed us by his blood (5:9-10, 12), appears as the canticle in the Evening Prayer of each Tuesday across all four weeks of the *Liturgy of the Hours*. It also appears in Evening Prayer II for the feast of the Exaltation of the Holy Cross (14 September), the feast of All Saints (1 November), Evening Prayer I for the feast of the Sacred Heart, and Evening Prayer II for the feast of Christ the King. The same selection is used for the celebration of Evening Prayer II in the Common of One and of Several Martyr(s).

The closing resurrection song of the seventh trumpet (11:17-18), coupled with song honoring the redeemed saints (12:10b-12a), appears as the canticle in the Evening Prayer of each Thursday across all four weeks of the *Liturgy of the Hours*. The same texts are used for Evening Prayer I and II for the feast of the Ascension, Evening Prayer I for the feast of the Body and Blood of Christ, and for Evening Prayer II on the feast of the Guardian Angels (2 October).

The song of Moses and the song of the Lamb (15:3-4) is widely used. It appears as the canticle for Evening Prayer on each Friday across all four weeks of the *Liturgy of the Hours*. It forms part of Evening Prayer II of the Epiphany of the Lord (6 January), Evening Prayer I for the feast of Pentecost, Evening Prayer II for the Dedication of a Church, for the Common of Pastors, and for the Common of Men Saints.

Finally, the rejoicing in heaven after the victory of the Lamb (19:1-2, 5-7) provides the canticle for Evening Prayer II of each Sunday of the *Liturgy of the Hours*. The same passage is used for Evening Prayer II for the celebration of Easter Sunday,

Pentecost Sunday, the feast of the Body and Blood of Christ, the feast of the Holy Trinity, Evening Prayer I for the Transfiguration of the Lord (6 August), All Saints, and Evening Prayer II for the feast of Christ the King. It provides the canticle for Evening Prayer I and II in the celebration of the Dedication of a Church during the Easter Season.

## Eucharistic celebrations

A similar focus upon the Easter message of Revelation is reflected in its use during the Liturgy of the Word in the Second (1:9-11a, 12-13, 17-19), Third (5:11-14), Fourth (7:9, 14b-17), Fifth (21:1-5a), Sixth (21:10-14, 22-23), and Seventh (22:12-14, 16-17, 20) Sundays of the Easter season in the Year C cycle of second readings.

As is well known, the feast of the Assumption of Our Lady (15 August) uses 11:19-12:6a, 10ab for its second reading, and the feast of All Saints (1 November) uses 7:2-4, 9-14. The presentation of the divine potential of humankind sits easily with a major celebration of the Mother of Jesus, as does the universal promise of salvation to Israel and all nations fittingly celebrate all the saints.

The victory of God over evil (20:11–21:1) and the description of life in the New Jerusalem (21:1-7) are used in Masses for the Dead. The acclamation marking the salvation of the faithful in Israel (14:3) also appears. Understandably, all these passages, in one way or another, are inspired by John's understanding of the perennial effects of the death and resurrection of Jesus.

A more traditional "end-time" interpretation appears to have led to the decision to locate the daily readings of Revelation from Monday of the Thirty-Third Week of the Ordinary Time of the Year to Saturday of the Thirty-Fourth Week in the Year 2 cycle. These first readings for daily celebrations of the Eucharist do not provide a continuous reading. However, a grasp of the overall narrative structure and message of the book should guide a pastor and the faithful through the readings selected.

Helpfully, although not continuous, these readings across the final weeks of Year 2 follow John's narrative across chapters 1 (vv. 1-4, 5-8), 2 (vv. 1-5a), 3 (vv. 1-6, 14-22), 4 (vv. 1-11), 5 (vv. 1-10), 10 (vv. 8-11), 11 (vv. 4-12), 14 (vv. 1-3, 4b-5, 14-19), 15 (vv. 1-4), 18 (vv. 1-2, 21-23), 19 (vv. 1-3, 9a), 20 (vv. 1-4; 20:11–22:2), and 22 (vv. 1-7). They might be liturgically located at the "end" of the liturgical year in the second cycle of daily readings, but almost all of them (chapters 1, 2, 11, 14, 15, 18, 19, 20) proclaim God's victory over evil. The final reading (22:1-7) informs believers that in the New Jerusalem they have received the living water and never-fading light of the Lord God.

In the *Liturgy of the Hours,* and in the texts chosen for the Liturgy of the Word during Eucharistic celebrations, the major focus of the liturgical readings in the Roman tradition is upon the Easter message of the book of Revelation. This holds true for the readings of the last weeks of Year 2, where the "end" of the year is in view. As that liturgical year runs down to its final celebration of the feast of Christ the King, the weekday readings remind us that the life and light we have received through our dwelling in the New Jerusalem (see 22:1-5) does not eliminate our hope in Jesus' promise of the final coming of the Lord Jesus (see 22:20).

# Works Cited

The studies listed below are only those works I have used in the brief footnotes that appear here and there throughout *Reading Revelation at Easter Time*. More copious bibliographies can be found in the major commentaries, especially in Koester, *Revelation*, 153–206, and in Moloney, *The Apocalypse of John*, 363–75.

## Commentaries

Aune, David E. *Revelation*. 3 vols. Word Biblical Commentary 52A-C. Dallas, TX: Word, 1997–1998.

Beale, G. K. *The Book of Revelation*. The New International Greek Testament Commentary. Grand Rapids: MI. Eerdmans, 1999.

Boring, M. Eugene. *Revelation*. Interpretation. Louisville, KY: John Knox Press, 1989.

Boxall, Ian. *The Revelation of Saint John*. Black's New Testament Commentaries. London: A&C Black, 2006.

Collins, Adela Y. *The Apocalypse*. New Testament Message 22. Wilmington, DE: Michael Glazier, 1979.

Koester, Craig R. *Revelation*. Anchor Yale Bible 38A. New Haven, CT: Yale University Press, 2014.

Lupieri, Edmondo F. *A Commentary on the Apocalypse of John*. Translated by Maria Poggi Johnson and Adam Kamesar. Italian Texts and Studies on Religion and Society. Grand Rapids, MI: Eerdmans, 2009.

Moloney, Francis J. *The Apocalypse of John. A Commentary*. Grand Rapids, MI: Baker Academic, 2020.

Prigent, Pierre. *Commentary on the Apocalypse of St. John*. Translated by Wendy Pradels. Tübingen: Mohr Siebeck, 2001.

Resseguie, James L. *The Revelation of John: A Narrative Commentary*. Grand Rapids, MI: Baker Academic, 2009.

## Other Studies

Attridge, Harold M. "Genre Bending in the Fourth Gospel." *Journal of Biblical Literature* 121 (2002): 1–21.

Bauckham, Richard. "Hades." Volume 3, pages 14–15 in David N. Freedman, ed., *The Anchor Bible Dictionary*. 6 vols. New York: Doubleday, 1992.

———. *The Climax of Prophecy: Studies in the Book of Revelation*. Edinburgh: T & T Clark, 1993.

———. *The Theology of the Book of Revelation*. New Testament Theology. Cambridge: Cambridge University Press, 1993.

Brown, Sherri, and Francis J. Moloney. *Interpreting the New Testament. An Introduction*. Grand Rapids, MI: Eerdmans, 2019.

Corsini, Eugenio. *The Apocalypse of John. The Perennial Revelation of Jesus Christ*. Eugene, OR: Wipf & Stock, 2019. Reprint of 1983 original.

Duffy, Eamon. "Brush for Hire. Lucas Cranach the Elder." In *Royal Books and Holy Bones. Essays in Medieval Christianity*, 301–18. London: Bloomsbury Continuum, 2018.

Foerster, Werner. "*oros*." In *Theological Dictionary of the New Testament*, volume 5, edited by Gerhard Kittel and Gerhard Friedrich, 475–87. Translated by Geoffrey W. Bromiley. Grand Rapids, MI: Eerdmans, 1964–76.

Friesen, Steven J. *Imperial Cults and the Apocalypse of John. Reading Revelation in the Ruins*. New York: Oxford University Press, 2001.

McGowan, Andrew B. *Ancient Christian Worship. Early Church Practices in Social, Historical, and Theological Perspective*. Grand Rapids, MI: Baker Academic, 2014.

McMullen, Ramsey. *Christianizing the Roman Empire (AD 100–400)*. New Haven, CT: Yale University Press, 1984.

Moloney, Francis J. *Belief in the Word. Reading John 1–4*. Minneapolis, MN: Fortress, 1993.

———. *The Gospel of Mark. A Commentary*. Grand Rapids, MI: Baker Academic, 2012.

Moyise, Steve. *The Old Testament and the Book of Revelation*. Supplements to the Journal for the Study of the New Testament 115. Sheffield: Sheffield Academic Press, 1995.

Pope Paul VI. *The Divine Office. The Liturgy of the Hours According to the Roman Rite*. 4 vols. New York: Catholic Book Publishing, 1976.

Stark, Rodney. *The Rise of Christianity. A Sociologist Reconsiders History*. Princeton, NJ: Princeton University Press, 1996.

Thackeray, H. St. J., Ralph Marcus, Allen Wikgren, and Louis H. Feldman, eds. *Josephus*. 9 vols. The Loeb Classical Library. Cambridge, MA/London: Harvard University Press/William Heinemann, 1926–1965.

Thompson, Leonard L. *The Book of Revelation. Apocalypse and Empire*. New York: Oxford University Press, 1990.

# Index of Authors